CAFÉ FRENCH

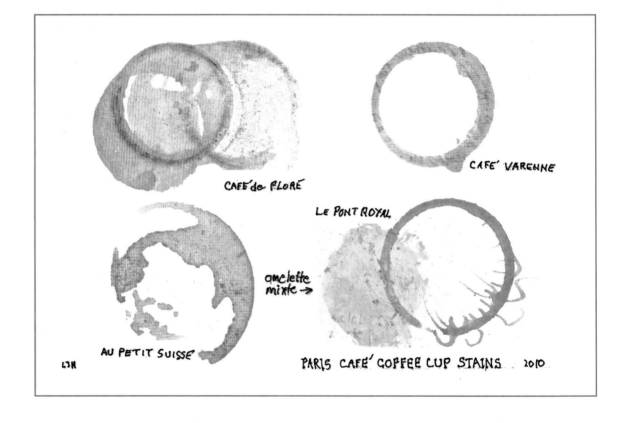

CAFÉ de FLORE

CAFÉ VARENNE

LE PONT ROYAL

omelette mixte →

AU PETIT SUISSE

LJH

PARIS CAFÉ COFFEE CUP STAINS   2010

Café French

A Flâneur's Guide to the Language, Lore and Food of the Paris Café

L. John Harris

Illustrated by the Author

Villa Books, Berkeley, California

ISBN 978-0-578-48537-9

Available on Amazon.com
www.ljohnharris.com

Villa Books
1569 Solano Ave. Suite 201
Berkeley, Ca., 94707

To my grandfather

Soloman Hirch Arekowitch

TABLE OF CONTENTS

I never rebel so much against France as not to regard Paris with a friendly eye; she has had my heart since my childhood…I love her tenderly, even to her warts and her spots. I am French only by this great city: the glory of France, and one of the noblest ornaments of the world.

– Michel de Montaigne

INTRODUCTION

Are you in love with Paris as much as I am? It's a condition, really, what the French might call an *amour fou* or "crazy love"—a radical, focused Francophilia that can take hold, sometimes, before one ever sets foot in the City of Light.

Do you yearn to inhabit, not merely frequent, Paris' charming sidewalk cafés, living the artful, romantic, almost mythic lifestyle portrayed in films, novels and the media? Perhaps you aspire, as I have, to be a *flâneur*, that iconic, ironic 19th-century Parisian type who raised urban strolling to an art form. In times past he was judged a lazybones and a loafer haunting the Grand Boulevards, arcades (*passages*) and cafés of Paris—the *boulevardier*. Later he became identified with a new breed of urban observer—the journalist. Later still, with the avant-garde poet, artist and *Belle Époch* decadent. Generally male, the flâneur, and now also the female *flâneuse*, was obsessed with the extraordinary, unequaled spectacle of Paris.

Here at home *aux États-Unis* we don't really stroll. Strolling requires a certain leisurely detachment, an aimlessness. In the U.S.A. aimlessness has been abolished. We steer our bodies towards our destination, our goal, our task. The target is usually to produce or consume, and as expeditiously as possible; seldom to just be, to linger, to observe. W. Scott Haine, a historian of France and author of books on café history, has described to me how he feels walking the streets of New York. "It seems to me that you have to combine the skills of ballet and broken-field running in order to negotiate the avenues of Gotham."

How many Francophile Americans—not to mention the English, Europeans generally and assorted others—have had the fantasy of a flâneur's café-culture lifestyle over the centuries of Paris' reign as Europe's cultural capital? How many have actually moved to Paris to cultivate that café lifestyle, to capture its relaxed (some would argue fading) *joie de vivre*? There are an estimated 30,000–100,000 (the U.S. Embassy no longer provides statistics) Americans in Paris today living the dream, despite the ups and downs of France's political, social and economic life. But you and I are not one of them, at least not yet. Can we nevertheless partake of the dream? Can we actually walk the flâneur's walk and talk the talk on our visits to Paris, rehearsing for the day we say, "Enough is enough, I'm moving to Paris"? The answer is, *Oui, bien sûr, absolument!* (Yes, of course, absolutely!)

Full disclosure: Despite the Parisian café's never-ending celebration in books, newspapers, magazines, films and blogs, the historic, artsy, even subversive Parisian café that we dream about—a Golden Age—is no more. The café of Paris' Enlightenment *philosophes*, revolutionary *citoyens*, strolling flâneurs, Impressionist painters, Belle Époch courtesans, *fin-de-siècle* decadents, modernist Surrealists and postmodern Situationists has been replaced by increasingly homogeneous—and often corporate-owned—cafés crowded with American bobos, Russian oligarchs, Middle Eastern oil tycoons, Asia's shopping elite and miscellaneous tourists from everywhere. The handful of historic cafés that remain do not always resemble the originals in form and function. Moreover, in reaction to the radical decline in the numbers of traditional cafés, many serving a modest neighborhood function, a new breed of café has emerged to meet the contemporary needs and tastes of remote-working, online millennials less interested in café joie than productivity—the bane of historic *flânerie*.

Nevertheless, we can channel the flâneur's lifestyle and, in the process, help to give new life to traditional cafés. In his introduction to *The Thinking Space: The Café as a Cultural Institution in Paris, Italy and Vienna*, W. Scott Haine gives us a useful formula:

Famous Paris literary cafés in particular have gained a second life after the actors have disappeared…They have become miraculous witnesses of a time past, and become places of pilgrimage that one visits like a museum with the secret hope of finding something of the lost time.

Yes, so true, but the hope is no secret! It is openly expressed by thousands of would-be flâneurs—and potential ex-pats—like you and me.

Caveat flâneur: Although *Café French* has some elements of a travel guide, such as a list of recommended cafés and some reviews, it is not a traditional guidebook. There are many excellent guides on the market (see Sources) that celebrate the cafés of Paris, tell their history and offer listings and reviews divided by category: literary and artist cafés, glamorous cafés, workers' cafés, tourist cafés, student cafés, internet cafés, etc. These often include seductive color photographs, sample menus, French language instruction and all the rest. My "guide," rather, is a very personal, perhaps peculiar and hopefully amusing (if not overtly instructive) exploration of the Paris café as a creative space, a place to discover oneself, one's dreams and even one's art in a convivial yet private social setting. One celebrated visitor cum resident in Paris, the

Irish artist George Moore, wrote in his *Confessions of a Young Man* (1888): "I did not go to either Oxford or Cambridge. . . But I went to the [Café de la] Nouvelle Athènes." Precisely my idea, too.

I began spending time in Paris in the late 1990s. Then, between 2011 and 2015, I was a Berkeley correspondent for the late online food journal *Zester Daily*. During that time, I spent at least a month in Paris each summer writing and illustrating articles, among them a series titled "Café French Lessons." I worked mostly in cafés near the apartments I was staying in, usually on the Left Bank. I used these cafés as my art and writing studio, my canteen and my flâneur's observation post, though I was not fully knowledgeable of the historic flâneur type when I started the series. I simply reflected on my life, my work and my dreams— and on the French language and history I was learning, the sights I was seeing, the streets I was strolling and the food I was tasting.

In one of my journal entries in 2013, I was already beginning to identify with the flâneur: "A flâneur in Paris! The humiliation of being a nobody is offset by the freedom of being a nobody." By the end of the Café French series in 2015, and after much delving into the growing scholarship on the flâneur, I began to believe that, subconsciously, I had been channeling him all along. Seated in my favorite cafés, usually

Brasserie Lipp
Blvd St. Germain

7/16/2000

A sketch at Brasserie Lipp from my journal in 2000. You can draw the back of heads without becoming conspicuous. I was thinking at the time of going back to art school, and maybe I should have! Instead, I began to revisit the culinary cartoons ("foodoodles") I had contributed to Bay Area food magazines in the 1990s. By 2010 I had a book of new cartoons and a memoir of my years working in and around Berkeley's notorious and self-proclaimed gourmet ghetto in the 70s and 80s—*Foodoodles: From the Museum of Culinary History.*

en terrasse, I scrutinized the world with an almost voyeuristic appetite: the endless stream of haute monde Parisians often accompanied by their fancy little dogs on leashes; the crush of tourists with their backpacks, maps, cameras and travel guides; university students on their funky bikes zipping through crowded streets filled with tiny cars; the pesky, pesty pigeons scavenging for scraps on the *trottoir* (sidewalk). The food, too, and the servers (*les garçons*) and chatty café-goers around me, oblivious to my scrutiny, all noted in my journal, grist for my mill and the products—illustrations and texts—that would appear in my magazine articles.

I had been fantasizing this life all my life, ever since, as a child, I had heard the stories of my Polish Jewish grandfather's stint during the 1890s in the French Foreign Legion, and the debt he felt to France not only for this "job" but later in San Francisco for the financial support he received from the local French community for his new business (textiles). Then came my first visit to Paris to see my brother and stay with his French family during his year abroad at the Sorbonne University in 1963. My eyes and taste buds opened to the glories of French food and art. This was a life, a world I loved and wanted to be part of.

In the articles I was writing about Paris and its cafés, a pattern began to emerge, a system I labeled

Another journal sketch, this one from 2012. One of my first encounters with bilingual homophonic confusion—the English "gout" (a disease) and the French *goût* (taste) and *goutte* (gout and drop)—the journal entry shows the mistakes I made with the phrase "*à chacun ses gouts*" (each to his own taste). The final drawing is in Lesson Seven. From sketchbook to printed book, the café artist-flâneur in action.

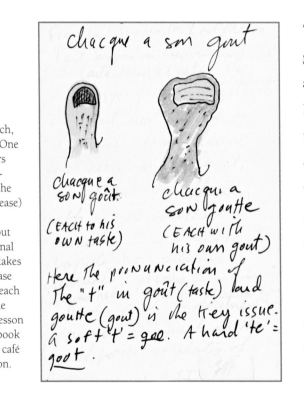

chacque a son gout

chacque a son goût.
(EACH to his OWN taste)

chacque a son goutte
(EACH with his own gout)

Here The pronunciation of The "t" in goût (taste) and goutte (gout) is the Key issue. a soft 't' = goo. A hard 'te' = goot.

"Café French." The word system suggests an unintended rigor—I am not a travel expert, let alone a philologist. No, this so-called system was simply the means by which I recorded in drawings and narrative, sometimes with tongue firmly in cheek, the process of absorbing just enough French and French culture to feel like a regular at my chosen cafés.

Along the way, I stumbled upon amusing word connections in French and English that caught my attention. These were the look- and/or sound-alike words that may or may not share a common meaning or etymology—the confusing linguistic world of cognates, homophones and bilingual *faux amis* (false friends). Writers use words to tell stories, but words often have surprising stories of their own. To tell mine, I have used my favorite discoveries in my texts and illustrations.

But you don't have to be a poet or artist to channel your inner flâneur. And you don't have to speak fluent French or live full time in Paris (I don't) to feel at home in a Parisian café (I do). What *is* essential, though, is careful observation. Any "art" that comes out of your observations is optional. The flâneur type may actually be, in my view, an inverted prototype of our contemporary performance artist who externalizes in public display his observations and ideas. For the flâneur, the performance is internalized in his imagination, a kind of strolling consciousness. At its root, the flâneur's work of art is himself, optionally translated into a preferred art medium. Or even, in our post-Duchampian, postmodern aesthetic universe, not at all.

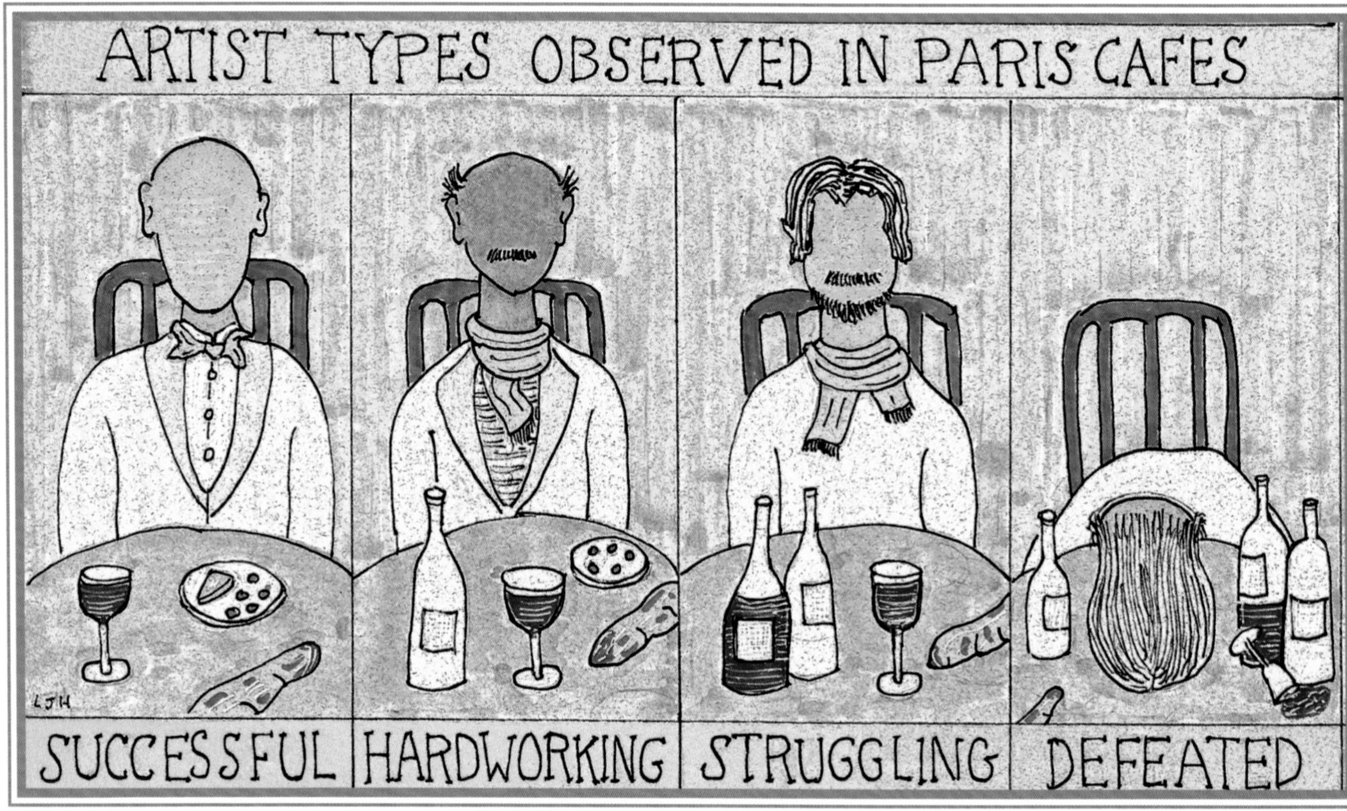
ARTIST TYPES OBSERVED IN PARIS CAFES
LJH
SUCCESSFUL
HARDWORKING
STRUGGLING
DEFEATED

The Flâneur and the Café

Thus the lover of universal life enters into the crowd as though it were an immense reservoir of electrical energy. Or we might liken him to a mirror as vast as the crowd itself; or to a kaleidoscope gifted with consciousness, responding to each one of its movements and reproducing the multiplicity of life and the flickering grace of all the elements of life.

– Charles Baudelaire
The Painter of Modern Life

The flâneur's very text inscribes his relationship to the city. . . the writer's own observations guarantee the authenticity of the text.

– Priscilla Parkhurst Ferguson
Paris as Revolution: Writing the 19th-Century City

It might seem counterintuitive, the idea of a flâneur's guide to Paris cafés. After all, the café is a place to sit, sometimes for hours, sipping a cup of coffee, eating a simple meal, reading the paper, sketching or writing in a journal, meeting with friends for conversation over a glass of wine, flirting with a date or just observing the passing crowd from the café's terrace, bathed in a marvelous shared privacy. On the other hand (or should I say foot?), historical flânerie, which dates back to the 16th and 17th centuries, is done by foot and alone, wandering aimlessly and anonymously about the city's crowded streets. The great French poet Charles Baudelaire referred to flânerie as "botanizing on the asphalt."

What binds the activity of the strolling flâneur and the passivity of the café-sitter is observation and the fuel that feeds both: caffeine and other liquid stimulants. Walter Benjamin, the early 20th-century German critic and champion of the flâneur's role in defining *modernisme*, described the streets and arcades of Paris circa 1840 as an "interior dwelling for the flâneur" who is "as much at home among the facades of houses as a citizen is in his four walls." Benjamin concludes that for the flâneur "the terraces of cafés are the balconies from which he looks down on his household after his work is done." (from "The Paris of the Second Empire in Baudelaire" in Walter Benjamin: *Selected Writings*).

Simply put, the observant café-goer is the working flâneur on a coffee break.

Cafés are the intermediate space between public exposure and the privacy of the home or workplace. But even flâneurs have to go home or back to work. The café is a way station for aesthetic gestation and fermentation, a "thirdspace" between work and home where observation and inspiration begin the transition to a finished work of art (a "capitalist commodity" in Benjamin's Marxist interpretation) completed in privacy.

From my Paris journal in 2015, the first version of my observation of the correlation between the amount of hair on male artists' heads, the amount of alcohol they consume and the level of their success. It seemed to me, at that moment, that the most elegant men—artists included—are often bald (natural or shaved), and that their success is on display in their restraint at table. They do not bury their pain (and failure) in excessive consumption of food and drink. Is this true? The letters "T," "P," "W" etc. stand for the colors (tan, pink, white) intended for the final drawing.

So what are would-be flâneurs to do when the historical conditions that created the synergy between flânerie and the café have vanished? We can fuel the "secret hope" that W. Scott Haine speaks of by studying *in situ* the Parisian cafés that have a claim to that history. There are historically significant, still-active cafés in Paris you will come across in the following pages, like Les Deux Magots, Café de Flore, Le Select, Café de la Paix, Le Procope and La Coupole, and many more with at least the feel of historical authenticity. By reading about cafés, especially *in* a café with a petit noir at hand, you are beginning the process of making it your own.

If you prefer (or just out of curiosity), you can join the young postmodern types, the millennial and post-millennial workers and bloggers, at one of the growing number of internet-friendly "co-working" cafés springing up all over Paris offering trendier beverages and foodstuffs in contemporary settings. They won't mind—as long as you pay by the hour! Focused on their computer screens and cell phones while "cyberflâneuring" the internet, these *start-uppers* won't even know you are there reading an actual book about the actual glories of the Paris café's actual past. *Triste à dire* (sad to say).

Likewise, one can study (and emulate, as I have tried to do) the 19th-century flâneur and the art of flânerie (from the verb *flâner*, to stroll). Strolling, however, is just the outward physical action of the true flâneur. For it is his convoluted consciousness that makes the flâneur what he really is: a detached, aestheticized observer—or anesthetized, if too much absinthe is consumed along the way. Either way, a critical eye. This is the view of flânerie popularized by Walter Benjamin through his studies of Charles Baudelaire, the quintessential 19th-century artist-flâneur. There are other ways of seeing the flâneur as he evolved from the wealthy idler in the early part of the 19th century through the end of the historic flâneur's reign in the Belle Époch, but Benjamin's perspective has been the most influential in shaping our current view of this cultural type.

The Benjaminian flâneur is not the Parisian boulevardier, dandy, libertine, decadent, rake or bohemian—all types which thrived in reaction to, even protest against, growing middle-class power, materialism and conformity following the French and Industrial revolutions. The flâneur's characteristics may overlap with these types, but he has his own distinctive qualities. "Anonymity to the point of invisibility was, in fact, the distinguishing marker of the flâneur as a formulaic character of popular culture," says cultural historian Mary Gluck in her fascinating book *Popular Bohemia: Modernism and Urban Culture in Nineteenth-Century Paris.*

The qualities of the flâneur are not achieved overnight, if ever they can be today. But if the historical flâneur is missing from the physical streets of Paris, he is increasingly present in spirit, as a metaphor for the kind of unrushed, intellectually rich and creative life we long for; and we can channel this spirit if we try. Paris showers its special magic on those who submit most fully to its siren call. That's the mission of today's flâneur.

Beware: The portrait I am painting of the flâneur is not the co-opted version found in contemporary commercial advertising and travel literature (i.e., the sophisticated bobo shopper). As with the other anti-bourgeois Parisian types I have mentioned—the dandy, the rake, the bohemian, the decadent—a romanticized image of the flâneur is used today to sell products, usually expensive ones. Ads abound featuring the flâneur (the Hermès brand), rakes (The Rake, a gentleman's "curated" fashion magazine published in London) and bohemians (boho couture). The fact that the much-coveted $1000-plus Louis Vuitton purse called the Lorette bag sports the lorette moniker, applied in the 19th century to low-level courtesans, many of whom lived near the Paris church Notre Dame de Lorette in the 9th, makes my point perfectly. It's not surprising that the Lorette bag's online marketing copy—"It's Louis Vuitton, it's girly and it's Marvelous"—says nothing about the darker origins of the term. Neither did the LV customer service rep I asked on the phone about the name's meaning.

Yes, the authentic flâneur "shops," but not for things.

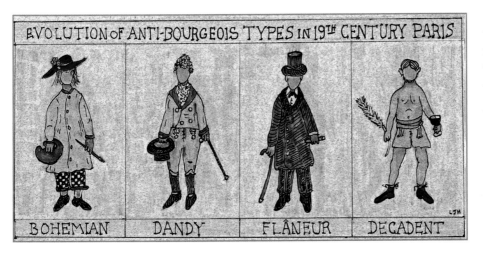

EVOLUTION of ANTI-BOURGEOIS TYPES in 19th CENTURY PARIS

BOHEMIAN — DANDY — FLÂNEUR — DECADENT

In order to blend or disappear into the crowd, the flâneur adopted the garb of the bourgeois male: the top hat, the black frock coat, the walking stick, even the cigar. Other types had the opposite impulse—to stand out. The difference between the early 19th-century boulevardiers and the later "incognito" flâneurs is that the former strolled around to attract attention, relying on flamboyant dress and a witty extrovert attitude.

THE ARTIST-FLÂNEUR

The flâneur is a seer, not a sightseer. I think of him—women were not yet free to flâner in the 19th century because, among other factors, they were thought to be unable to achieve the emotional detachment necessary for flânerie—as an "inside outsider." After my first few Parisian summer *séjours* (extended stays), as I began to learn more about this character, I realized that the life I sought in Paris was as much *inside* my own head as *outside* in the streets, shops, cafés, parks and museums I was visiting. The more I read the more I tried to model the behavior and style. Being alone in Paris for months at a time, I certainly felt the anonymity that the flâneur cultivates, no matter the friendships that developed for me in Paris. *Petit à petit* (little by little) I was becoming *un vrai* (true) *flâneur*, or so it felt. I am not the bohemian or decadent of my 20s and 30s, nor am I the rake or dandy of my 40s, 50s and 60s. The flâneur seems to fit me now, in my early 70s.

Baudelaire, Walter Benjamin's ultimate flâneur, flirted with the dandy type throughout his life, but Edgar Allan Poe's "The Man of the Crowd" was a more powerful attraction. In Poe's story, the unnamed narrator follows another man (the man of the crowd) he has noticed from his café seat and observes him in the context of the swirling action of London's streets. Poe's narrator is the prototype of the detective, a private eye sussing out the city's secrets and hidden crimes. Baudelaire, as reflected in his great collection of poems, *Les Fleurs du Mal*, provides the somewhat subversive/paranoid tint that colors Benjamin's view of the flâneur as the transgressive modern (avant-garde) artist—the artist-flâneur.

From Baudelaire's poem "Artist Unknown":

No illustrious tombstones ornament
    the lonely churchyard where I often go
to hear my heart, a muffled drum, parade
    incognito.

Compared to Baudelaire, you can describe me as artist-flâneur-lite.

THE CAFÉ AS DREAMING SPACE

When he was not "drinking in with his eye" (Honoré de Balzac's description of the flâneur's project) the commercial arcades of early to mid-19th-century Paris and the new boulevards of Baron Haussmann's reconstructed Paris during the Second Empire, the flâneur was adding his special presence to the cafés he inhabited. These functioned as what Scott Haine has termed "the thinking space." In the 18th and 19th centuries the Paris café was an important contributor to the democratization of France and a provocative model for cafés all over Europe. More than any other institution, the café invited people of all social strata (and eventually of all races and genders, though exceptions exist even today) to express their most radical and private thoughts in a public space. It had replaced the royal court and high society salon as a place to argue aesthetic, philosophical and political ideas, no matter how scandalous. And there was relatively little risk of arrest or challenge by government agents. The café was a caffeinated "cabal," as one 19th-century observer noted.

For me the café is primarily a dreaming space. Before we can think freely, speak freely and create freely we must dream freely. Perhaps "daydreaming" is a better term, because when I'm in a café I'm definitely not asleep, though napping is not unknown in cafés. Reverie is perhaps an even better word for the kind of mental activity that precedes creative expression. In *The Poetics of Space*, the great French phenomenologist Gaston Bachelard presents an extraordinary and challenging examination of this pre-creative dream state triggered by, and colored by, the various rooms of a home. The café is, of course, a symbolic extension of the home, a place of "intimate solitude," says Professor Haine, my go-to authority on the history and function of Parisian cafés.

I think it's the dreaming function of the café that can connect café-goers today to their inner flâneur. It may be too late to experience cafés in the same way that Voltaire and Verlaine, Baudelaire and de Beauvoir, and Monet and Modigliani did, but it's never too late to dream.

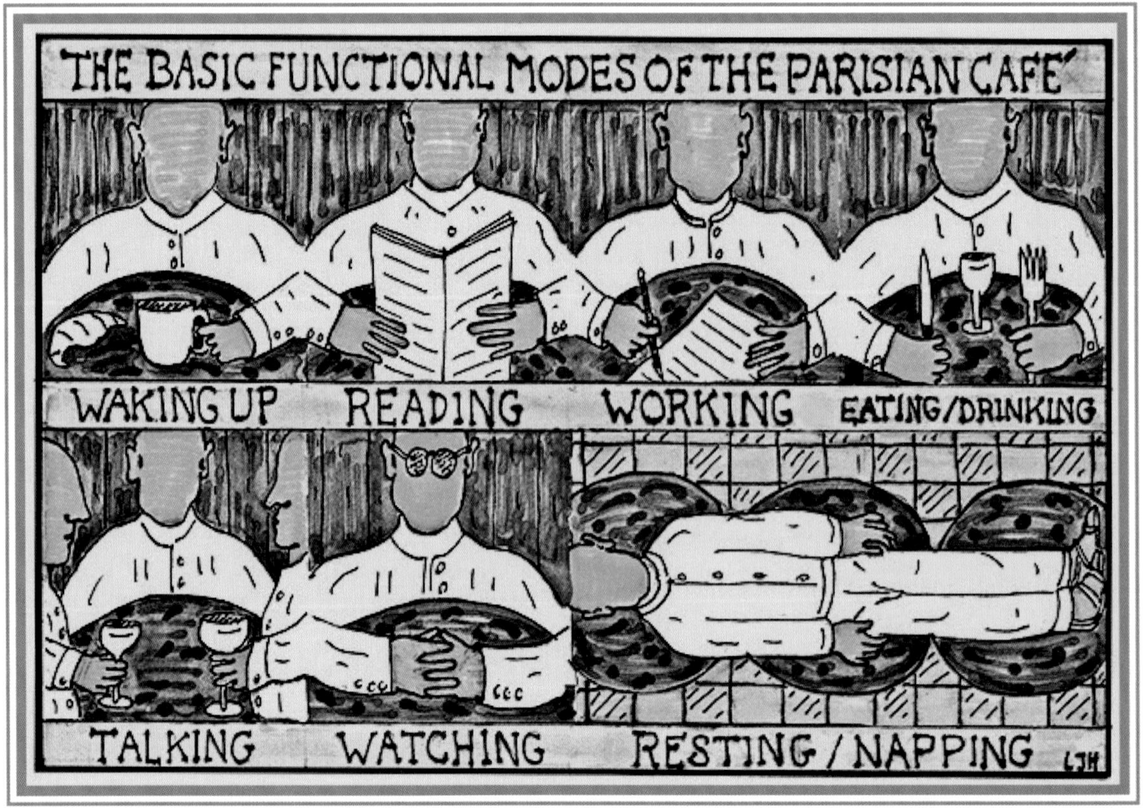
"THE BASIC FUNCTIONAL MODES OF THE PARISIAN CAFÉ"
WAKING UP
READING
WORKING
EATING/DRINKING
TALKING
WATCHING
RESTING / NAPPING
LJH

THE CAFÉ IS DEAD, LONG LIVE THE CAFÉ!

Alone on the outdoor terrace I studied my foot-long baguette sandwich. . . Beyond, through the misty keyhole view, were the tin-covered gabled roofs and distant spires of the city bathing in native sepia. I devoured the atmosphere. The sandwich seemed secondary.

– David Downie
A Taste of Paris

When the traditional Paris café is featured in books and other media, it's most often in relation to its function as a casual eating and drinking venue, the café as bar, bistro, brasserie and restaurant. The other uses of the café as a workspace or flâneurian observation post are secondary. (However, "people watching" is often mentioned.) These days the reviews are not too encouraging. We are told by food writers about bitter brews, perfunctory pâtés, questionable quiches, catastrophic croques (see Lesson Twelve), insipid salads, chewy chicken (see Lesson Thirteen) and tepid tarts (and I don't mean the lorettes of yore!), all served by grumpy garçons.

This is just the culinary dimension of the café's contemporary woes. Other factors are putting Paris' traditional cafés at risk, including rising commercial rents in gentrified neighborhoods and the attraction of more contemporary cafés better aligned with the social media habits and Wi-Fi needs (pronounced wee-fee in French) of young Parisians and visitors.

These social, political and economic issues require serious attention and action, and they're getting both from activist groups like Save the Paris Café, founded by Lisa Anselmo, author of *My (Part-Time) Life in Paris: How Running Away Brought Me Home*. However, I have found it instructive as a sometime food journalist to place the challenges of the traditional café's food into the larger context of the "bad press" French gastronomy has encountered over the last few decades.

Paris' alleged decline as the world capital of white-tablecloth "fine dining" has been well documented in the media, and the Parisian café has followed close behind, its tail between its legs. Frozen and packaged food and off-premises preparation in restaurants has sparked a strong reaction from the French government. Since 2015, a *fait maison* designation ("made on premises") is displayed in the windows of dining establishments that meet the standard. Still, a recent article states that a high percentage of Paris dining establishments serve frozen and/or preprepared industrial foods. Something to think about the next time you tuck into that tasteless coq au vin you've crossed the Atlantic for!

Back in 2014, while I was in the middle of the Café French Lessons series for my magazine, a report from food writer Mark Bittman in the *New York Times*, "French Food Goes Down," shook the international foodie world with its downbeat assessment. London, Hong Kong, Copenhagen, Barcelona and, stateside, New York and San Francisco had emerged, wrote Bittman, as competing, if not transcendent centers of *haute cuisine.* But Bittman and others before him, like Michael Steinberger in *Au Revoir to All That: The Rise and Fall of French Cuisine*, were a bit early to French cuisine's funeral. The outlook for Paris and France was already brightening as Bittman was penning his eulogy, with critics like Nicholas Lander noting in the *Financial Times* a "renaissance of fine dining in Paris."

As David Downie puts it so colorfully in his recent book, *A Taste of Paris: A History of the Parisian Love Affair with Food*, "Declinist pathology is endemic in France and has spread to the New World where American critics have raised their cudgels and beaten French food to a pulp." Yet, he adds, "the food and wine of Paris are more varied and better than at any other time in the last forty years, since I've known the city."

There is even talk now of a neoclassical revival of traditional French cuisine in culinary capitals around the globe, proving the point, I believe, that French cuisine, while experiencing many up and down cycles over the centuries, always ends up . . .up.

JOIE DE STARBUCKS

Though the rumors of French cuisine's demise are greatly exaggerated, to paraphrase Mr. Twain, the Paris café's non-gastronomic problems are real and serious. According to the Save the Paris Café website, the number of cafés in Paris has shrunk from 45,000 in 1880 to only about 7,000 today. Save the Paris Cafe is setting itself the task of halting this slide towards oblivion. The organization's website states the goal:

> *We seek to celebrate what's special about café culture, work with café owners to help them innovate with the times and remain relevant—and encourage city government to support local business owners, preserving cafés by helping them thrive.*

Sign me up!

The operative term here is "relevant," and for me this means internet access, not just better coffee and freshly made artisanal foods. I became particularly aware of this issue of relevance when I looked for a café with an available Wi-Fi signal in the summer of 2015. I wanted to conduct an email interview in real time between Paris and Berkeley. It was apparent that traditional Parisian café owners at that time would rather close up shop than give out their Wi-Fi passwords.

One afternoon I had to swallow my pride. None of the Montparnasse cafés I was frequenting had signal access, so I asked at a newspaper kiosk where I could find a café with Wi-Fi and was directed to Starbucks. *Mon Dieu!* I would have to swallow not only my pride, but also their "handcrafted lattes" (served in paper cups, of course), which are no better in Paris than in the U.S.

I was trying to connect with my friend Leonard Pitt, the Berkeley-based author of *Walks Through Lost Paris: A Journey into the Heart of Historic Paris*, a fascinating illustrated guide to Baron Haussmann's extraordinary mid-19th-century transformation of Paris and its regrettable by-product, the destruction of so much of Paris' charmingly medieval cityscape. I wanted to know Lenny's views of Parisian café culture then—when he lived in Paris in the 1960s—and now. He was to respond from his computer at the café in Berkeley's

French Hotel (now the SenS Hotel), across the street from the legendary Cal/French restaurant and café, Chez Panisse. Chez Panisse is Berkeley's heartfelt and internationally recognized expression of love for Provençal French cooking translated into a culinary California Arts & Crafts vernacular.

Working from my computer at the dreaded Starbucks Odéon, the setup seemed a bit surreal. Conversing with Lenny via computer, he at the American-based French Hotel café and I in Paris at an American-owned chain outlet (I just cannot label Starbucks a café) gave the exchange an absurd gravitas that makes me smile to this day.

Lenny is a passionate proponent of a café-centric lifestyle he posits against the Protestant work ethic of a Puritanized America. He is also passionate about the eternal beauty of Paris and works closely with the International Coalition for the Preservation of Paris, an organization whose mission is to resist new developments that would dwarf the incomparable and relatively low Paris skyline with a ring of giant skyscrapers around the picturesque *centre* of Paris—the heart of Paris that gave rise to café culture in the first place, and to the flâneurs that have strolled there ever since.

Lenny emailed me that "Nothing better symbolizes the congeniality, the rhythm and sheer joie de vivre we ache to recapture in life than the café." Well put, Pitt! But one man's joie de vivre is another man's (or woman's) morning coffee ritual, writing or art studio, afternoon or evening gathering spot for conversation and nourishment or flâneur's solo observation post. And often, all the above and more. The traditional Parisian café is more than the sum of its parts.

SOME OF ITS PARTS

The cafés I adopted on my recent stays in Paris, mostly in the heart of the café-rich 6th arrondissement's Latin Quarter—which spills over from its heart in the 5th—provide the perfect vantage point for reflections on the traditional café's basic functions. (See page 29, My Paris Café Index.)

WAKE UP (*SE RÉVEILLER*) AND SMELL THE COFFEE

When I go to a Paris café to wake up with a café crème, the least important criteria for me are the coffee's origin, quality or even, I confess, taste. The ubiquitous Cafés Richard brand of coffee served all over Paris does not make a very good cup, but at 7 a.m. I don't really care (See Lesson Fourteen on Balzac and the bifurcation of coffee's taste and function). My legs may get me to the café, but my critic's brain is still on snooze. This particular summer I began most days at my *café du coin* (neighborhood café), Café Madame. There is nothing exceptional about Café Madame—they serve a typical *petit déjeuner* with passable coffee, acceptable croissant or buttered *tartine*, and reasonably fresh orange juice)—except for its convenient proximity to my apartment and the Luxembourg Gardens nearby, a flâneur's dreamscape.

WORKING (*TRAVAILLER*): READING (*LIRE*), WRITING (*ÉCRIRE*), SKETCHING (*FAIRE DES CROQUIS*)

After my morning coffee and a short stroll through the Luxembourg Gardens, I would arrive back at my apartment awake and ready for work (i.e., reading, writing and sketching). Later I would head out again to another café for lunch and more work. The late morning's first round of work at home is often devoted to reviewing and refining the work done at the café the preceding day or night. In the afternoon I tend to sit in cafés and go into reverie mode, a combination of outward observation and inward free-association or "woolgathering." This is when images and thoughts come together for future sketches and/or texts.

Any café can be a working café, depending on one's personal requirements. Kaaren Kitchell, an expat novelist, poet and blogger (*Paris Play*), combines her daily one-hour walk with her writing and editing projects, so her café must be at least a thirty-minute walk from home. Her other criteria include a quiet ambiance and, ergo, few tourists. "The French know how to modulate their voices," says Kitchell, "Americans and Italians don't."

On the other hand, expat author (*Paris Par Hasard: From Bagels to Brioche*), tour guide and *bon vivant* Terrance Gelenter prefers to work in crowded, noisy cafés like Les Deux Magots and Café Montorgueil. His previous reign at Café Le Select ended when the management suggested he move on. Says Gelenter, "Once we grew to twenty happy, good-tipping Americans we became *personae non gratae*."

Every Sunday from 11 a.m. to 1 p.m. Gelenter holds "office hours" for his tour clients and visiting Anglophone writers, artists, filmmakers and the like. It may not seem like work when you meet with him at his usual outdoor table, but he is definitely working the terrace. He is very gifted at it, I might add.

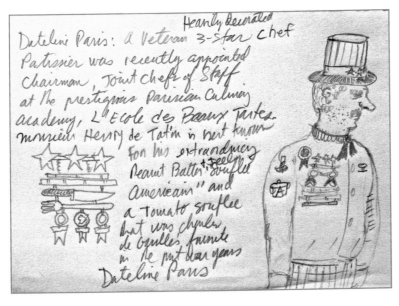

I've always been intrigued by the uniform worn by "the French chef" and its historic ties to clerical and military uniforms. In fact, the French *chef de cuisine*'s kitchen staff has been called the *brigade* since Auguste Escoffier's time. In this sketch I'm imagining the merger of the French chef and the American military's Chairman, Joint Chiefs of Staff— Chairman, Joint Chefs of Staff.

Sometimes he even breaks into Sinatra tunes. His newsletter, *The Paris Insider*, offers travel tips, author interviews, a calendar of arts events, and hotel, restaurant and book reviews.

CONVERSATION (*PARLER, DISCUTER, PAPOTER*)

Where better than at a café to have a conversation? Dating back to its origins in the late 17th century, the Paris café has inhabited a middle world between public and private space where, unlike at more food-focused bistros and brasseries, spirited inter-table discourse is welcome, if not required. This "free speech movement" was not invented in Berkeley in 1964. For the 18th-century dramatists and philosophers and 19th-century Impressionists who broke with the stifling constraints of the Academy, the café became a salon where artists could engage freely in debates over aesthetic issues—with the help, of course, of sufficient, if not addictive, amounts of coffee, wine and, more euphorically, absinthe and even opium. Talk about Happy Hour (pronounced *app*-ee ower, like Eisenhower), which these days begins in cafés and pubs as early as mid-afternoon.

However, one early 20th-century artist and café-goer, the monumental Marcel Duchamp, has presented an amusingly contrarian view of the café's conversation function. He is quoted by Calvin Tomkins in *Marcel Duchamp: The Afternoon Interviews*:

> *In the case of the Impressionists it could be a very useful thing—one artist would say a word that caught the imagination of the others, that's true. But it's a very, very artificial thing . . . full of new words and flourishing language and so forth, but no actual exchange and no understanding of the other one's ideas.*

The notoriously tight-lipped Duchamp famously abandoned art and art talk when in mid-career he withdrew into the silence of chess competition. Chess, it should be noted, was an important activity in many 18th- and 19th-century cafés. But for me, and no doubt for most regulars who do their work in cafés, meeting friends for conversation in the afternoon after work sessions is a ritual I place on the same high level as the flâneurian strolls that bring me there.

One final note regarding the café's role in the highly-evolved French art of seduction (*la séduction*) and its verbal dimension. While on a flâneurian stroll from my apartment on rue Madame towards boulevard Saint-Germain I walked past the Village Voice Bookshop just before it was to sadly close its doors in July of 2012. An author, *New York Times* writer Elaine Sciolino, was giving a reading from her new book, *La Seduction: How the French Play the Game of Life*. I wandered in and of course bought the book, hoping to glean secrets that might provide an amorous summer diversion from my flâneurian solitude. Here is how Ms. Sciolino describes the relationship between conversation and seduction, second in importance only, she professes, to *le regard* (the seductive look or glance):

The word is the second weapon. Verbal sparring is crucial to French seduction, and conversation is often less a means of giving or receiving information than a languorous mutual caress.

I will keep this in mind while on my next café date.

WATCHING (*OBSERVER*)
AND RESTING/NAPPING (*SE REPOSER/FAIRE LA SIESTE*)

In Lesson One I focused on the observational function of the café and its connection to flânerie. It's as if the café was destined for "the eminently Parisian compromise between laziness and activity known as flânerie!" This drollery by Victorien Sardou, quoted in Edmund White's book *The Flâneur: A Stroll through the Paradoxes of Paris (Writer and the City)*, sums up the high regard for lounging and loafing in a bygone era before commercial productivity became Western civilization's highest value. The flâneur challenged the modern trope of productivity that turned workers into cogs in a machine.

As for the café's function as an urban resting place, it is a tourist's necessity after days filled with shopping and sightseeing. The café's napping function is, I admit, a conceptual stretch. Although traditional cafés still tolerate long stays and minimal consumption, I don't think they would tolerate napping. Certainly not the high-end cafés, which drive off flâneurs as early as 11 a.m. under the pretext that the tables must be set for luncheon.

Nevertheless, while at Les Deux Magots one afternoon, I sketched three tables pulled together with a man sleeping on top—a visual punch line to my multipaneled drawing. A nap must have been on my To Do list. Come to think of it, for us older flâneurs, this is not such a bad idea. Imagine, traditional cafés with cots in napping sections paid for by the hour! With increasing numbers of young café-goers heading to trendy coworking cafés, maybe there could now be room, and a profit incentive, for traditional café owners. To my friends at Save The Paris Café, are you listening?

Summing up the functions of the Parisian café, and depending on one's needs—whether tourist, artist, working professional, student studying for exams, mother with hungry children or first-date flirters—the café is a home away from home, an office away from the office, a study hall, a restaurant for nourishment and celebration, a bar for drinks and flirtation, or just an observation post for thinking, dreaming and resting. Napping is optional.

À chacun son café!

MY PARIS CAFÉ INDEX

These are the cafés I visited while on one of my summer Café French sabbaticals. Most are in the 6th. According to my notes, I made fifty-six visits to the twenty-six cafés listed. That's about two café visits per day, just the right pace for a practicing flâneur in Paris.

Café des Beaux-Arts, 7 Quai Malaquais, 6th
Café Bonaparte, 42 rue Bonaparte, 6th
Bread & Roses, 7 rue de Fleurus, 6th
Café Cassette, 73 rue de Rennes, 6th
Les Deux Magots, 6 Place Saint-Germain, 6th
Café de Flore, 172 blvd. Saint-Germain, 6th
Café de Fleurus, 2 rue de Fleurus, 6th
La Fontaine, 20 rue Cuvier, 5th
Le Hibou, 16 Carrefour de l'Odeon, 6th
Café l'Horizon, 120 rue de Rennes, 6th
Le Luxembourg, 58 blvd. Saint-Michel, 6th
Café Madame, 25 rue de Vaugirard, 6th
Café de la Mairie 8 Place Saint-Sulpice, 6th

Café du Métro, 67 rue de Rennes, 6th
Le Nemours, 2 Place Colette, 1st
Le News Café, 78 rue d'Assas, 6th
Café la Palette, 43 rue de Seine, 6th
Les Petites Gouttes, 12 Esp. N. Sarraute, 18th
Au Petit Suisse, 16 rue de Vaugirard, 6th
Le Petite Luxembourg, 29 rue de Vaugirard, 6th
Les Philosophes, 28 rue Vieille du Temple, 4th
Le Pré aux Clercs, 30 rue Bonaparte, 6th
Le Royal Opéra, 19 Avenue de l'Opéra, 1st
Le Select, 99 blvd. du Montparnasse, 6th
Café Vavin, 18 rue Vavin, 6th
Le Café Zéphyr, 12 blvd. Montmartre, 9th

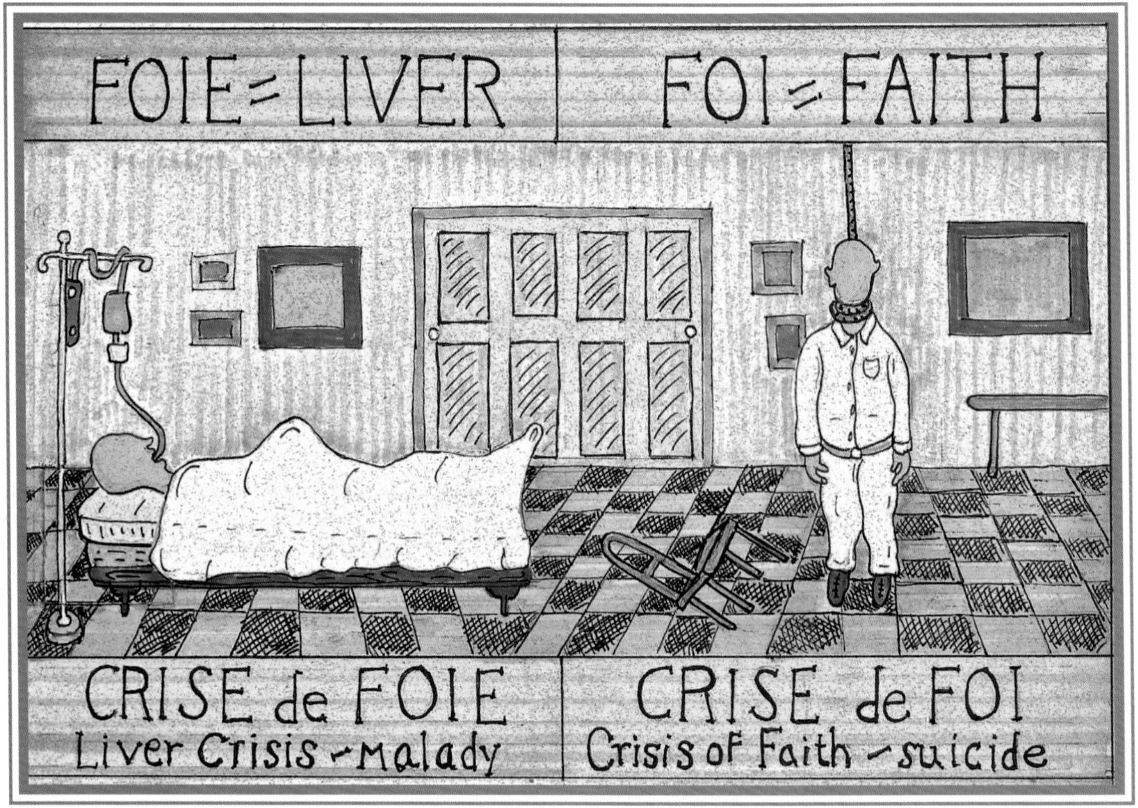
FOIE = LIVER
FOI = FAITH
CRISE de FOIE
Liver Crisis - Malady
CRISE de FOI
Crisis of Faith - suicide

LIVER, BAD FAITH AND TIME

Dialectics, matrices, archetypes all need to connect once in a while, back to some of that proletarian blood, to body odors and senseless screaming across a table, to cheating and last hopes, or else all is dusty Dracularity, the West's ancient curse.

– Thomas Pynchon
Gravity's Rainbow

The many varied functions of the café should be placed in their historical context. This centuries-old social and gastronomic institution derives its name from the Arabic word for coffee, *qahwa,* via the Turkish *kahve.* The oldest café still operating in Paris (and the second to open), Le Procope, where the likes of Voltaire, Diderot, Robespierre and Napoleon were served, dates back to 1686. It functions today mainly as a tourist brasserie, though Parisians still do come for lunch at the Procope. Although venerable cafés continue to attract creative types and would-be flâneurs like yours truly, the traditional French café is in crisis, both existential and gastronomical. Crisis (*crise,* pronounced kreez) will be the theme of this lesson.

American author and critic Adam Gopnik, perhaps our most exuberantly articulate Francophile, has dubbed the French café the "highest embodiment of French commonplace civilization." The café, he seems to be saying, is so embedded in quotidian French life that for the French it simply *is.* And many French would say, "Crisis be damned!" (*Au diable!*). If things were only that simple.

A CRISE DE FOIE (LIVER)

To echo Gopnik, while the Parisian café is arguably the highest embodiment of the French café (it's in Paris after all), the numbers are, as previously noted, dwindling at an alarming rate. So what's behind the decline, other than socioeconomic and food quality considerations? In part, I propose, health concerns.

Consider: The food consumed at a Parisian café, whether good, bad or indifferent, is not by any stretch of the imagination "health food." This may not be as much a concern for the French as it is for tourists, especially Americans. It might be an exaggeration to say that abusing the traditional Parisian café can kill you, but for the uninitiated it may not be far from the truth. Think about it: all the glorious French consumables associated with the café are either high in alcohol (wine, absinthe); caffeine (coffee, tea); butterfat (croissants and cheeses) and sugar (pastries and tarts); and animal fat and salt (charcuterie, foie gras). This is French gastronomic heaven translated into nutritional Russian roulette, at least for the health obsessed.

Let's focus for a moment on *foie gras* (pronounced fe-wah *grah*), that quintessential Gallic delicacy that translates as "fattened liver." It is made from the enlarged livers of ducks (*canard*) and geese (*oie*, pronounced *wha*). Eighty-five percent of the calories in foie gras are from fat. As delicious as it is, woe to the tourist who would gorge on fattened duck livers!

Usually found at cafés in the form of a spreadable mixture, *pâté de foie gras de canard* (or *oie*) is served with slices of toasted bread and small pickles called *cornichons*. The real deal (whole or *entier*) is, of course, more expensive and is best when semi-cooked (*mi-cuit*).

Like the Parisian café itself, foie gras is also in crisis. The controversial process of manufacturing foie gras—force-feeding corn to ducks and geese to fatten their livers (the technique of *gavage*, see illustration)—has been challenged in the United States where periodically animal welfare activists manage to shut down this age-old process, if not the *consumption* of imported foie gras, which remains legal. In France, where such questions have greater relevance, there is a growing concern about duck and goose welfare and the production of foie gras. But Francophile foie gras lovers need not panic just yet. France remains essentially a rural, agricultural society, and its gastronomic traditions are seemingly unbreakable even when sorely tested.

GAVAGE = GAVAGE

CRISE du CANARD
CRISIS of the DUCK

Gavage in English also refers to the technique of feeding newborn infants having problems swallowing milk or formula by inserting a tube down their nose and into their stomach. No protest here. It's a lifesaving procedure.

Just as stuffing feed into birds can enlarge their livers to near bursting, the same is true for gourmands who feast on those very same livers. Foie gras consumption, combined with fatty meats, rich desserts, buttery cheeses and an abundance of wine can unleash what the French call a *crise de foie*, literally a "crisis of the liver." From mild symptoms of dyspepsia (indigestion) to acute bilious conditions, such liver maladies (*les maladies du foie*) can be serious, even fatal.

The liver is not the only organ to suffer the assaults of animal fat associated with classic French food. While it appears that "enlarged" gastronomes of the past could get away with the excessive indulgences of *la grande cuisine*—obesity was a sign of prosperity and walking after meals still existed before the automobile age, somewhat offsetting gluttonous abandon—the modern era's rotund gourmets and gourmands on both sides of the Atlantic have not fared as well.

A few names come to mind in this regard. The "prince" of gourmets, Curnonsky (real name Maurice Edmond Sailland, 1872–1956), who topped the scales at 277 pounds, died in his 80s while on a diet, though his death is reported as a fall from a window—possibly the result of calorie-denied fainting. The American writer and Francophile gastronome A. J. Liebling (1904–1963) lived a gluttonously pleasurable (when not covering a war) but abbreviated life, suffering from heart and kidney disease and painful chronic gout. James Beard (1903–1985), the 300-pound-plus heavyweight of American gastronomy, lived to a surprising 81 but suffered enormously from gout and other degenerative diseases. Jeremiah Tower, the cocreator of California cuisine in Berkeley and San Francisco and a devoted Beard acolyte, reports in his tell-all autobiography, *California Dish: What I Saw (and Cooked) at the American Culinary Revolution*, the routines of massaging and bandaging Beard's swollen feet and the maroon and black color of his legs, all "devastated by a lack of circulation."

Of course, if you could go back in time and ask these long-suffering gastronomers if they regretted their painfully consequential gluttony, I'm sure they would roar in unison, "Not one calorie! Now where's my napkin?"

CRISE DE FOI (FAITH)

It is curious, if not confusing, that the French word for liver, *foie*, is phonetically identical to the French word for faith (*foi*). A *crise de foi* (crisis of faith) is usually associated with a religious crisis, e.g., the belief that God is dead. However, in French *existentialisme*, the 20th-century philosophical school most identified with celebrated Deux Magots regulars Jean-Paul Sartre, Simone de Beauvoir, Albert Camus and others, one's crise de foi may be secular in nature. The sufferer feels that life is meaningless and absurd. Related to this condition is the "bad faith"—Sartre's *mauvaise foi*—of false values and inauthentic action. This existential crisis can lead to extreme acts of political, artistic and psychological violence, even suicide (the same in French, pronounced su-ee-*seed*). Which leads to one of the darker functions of the Parisian café: a place to

café de la Mairie/Salpeas

Isolated Café-goers at the bar

Café
Le News @ Rue d'Assas
sound track in English
Cafés Richard 6-26-14

be depressed in. Downcast portraits of café-goers by artists such as Van Gogh, Degas, Toulouse-Lautrec and Picasso are ubiquitous. (See Lesson Eight for more on the related condition of *ennui*, a profound boredom bordering on depression.)

ONE MORE FOIS (TIME)

One more "fe-*wah*" to consider: the word for time (*fois*) as in "for a second time" or "the next time." So, for example, if your first attempt at suicide fails, you can try again for a second time—*une deuxième fois*. Or, if you are hospitalized for a crise de foie, you might be more cautious when eating pâté de foie gras the next time—*la prochaine fois*.

In my experience, spending months at a time flâneuring in Paris, studying and living the art of the café, I have never experienced, other than short-lived bouts of ennui, a true crise—existential, gastroenterological or otherwise. Only on occasion that bittersweet feeling of contentment (*le contentement*) tinged with nostalgia (*la nostalgie*) the French describe as *la vie en rose* (life in the pink).

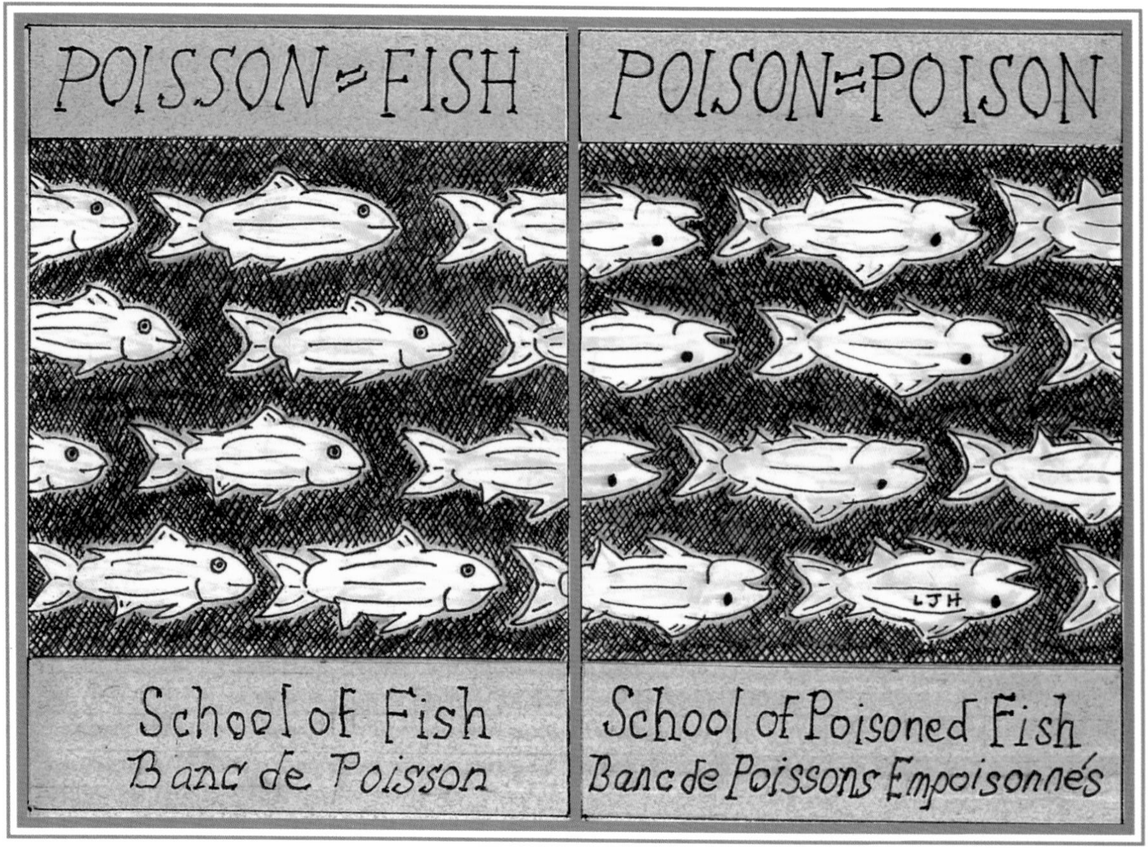
POISSON = FISH
POISON = POISON
LJH
School of Fish
Banc de Poisson
School of Poisoned Fish
Banc de Poissons Empoisonnés

Fish, Poison and James Beard's Fork

Bouillabaisse, this golden soup, this incomparable golden soup which embodies and concentrates all the aromas of our shores and which permeates, like an ecstasy, the stomachs of astonished gastronomes.

– Curnonsky
Traditional Recipes of the Provinces of France

One key to mastering the art of the café lifestyle in Paris is to be aurally vigilant and verbally precise. Embedded in the French language are gastro-linguistic time bombs just waiting to explode. Did your French garçon just call Sainte Anne, Paris' largest psychiatric hospital, because you ordered poison (*poison*, pronounced pu-wah-*zon*) instead of fish (*poisson*, pronounced pu-wah-*son*)? The French pronunciation rule here is that a single "s" appearing between two vowels—"i" and "o" in the case of poison—is pronounced "z." And a double "ss" appearing between two vowels, as in poisson, is pronounced "ss."

SOMETHING'S FISHY HERE

There may be reason enough in our polluted world to worry about being poisoned by fish without ordering it that way! Which begs the question: Where does Paris actually get its fish? Where do the restaurants in Paris serving southern French dishes like the classic Marseille bouillabaisse get their shellfish and rockfish? Where do your café's oysters (*les huîtres*), mussels (*les moules*), scallops (*les coquilles Saint-Jacques*) and tuna (*le thon*) come from? Hundred-mile locavores take note: Paris is a long way from its Atlantic and Mediterranean coasts. While the river Seine and smaller rivers and streams around Paris were once sources of freshwater fish, this is no longer the case due to industrial pollution, especially from nuclear power plants. Even with its spectacular ocean bounty, France today is a net importer of seafood, according to reports I've seen.

But despite discouraging trends in French cuisine (see Lesson Three) much of the gastronomic apparatus that made France the envy of the Western world over the last several centuries remains intact.

THE GASTRONOMIC REACH OF PARIS

It was the one and only Curnonsky who christened Paris both a "tentacular" city and the digesting "belly" of France. Gastronomic France was conceptualized as a huge wheel with spokes that radiated out from the hub: Paris. And like some gourmandizing Goliath, Paris reached out over *la France profonde* (deep rural France) to rake in the regional treasures of its incomparably fertile terroir.

You might say that culinary Paris in the first half of the 20th century was embodied by Curnonsky himself.

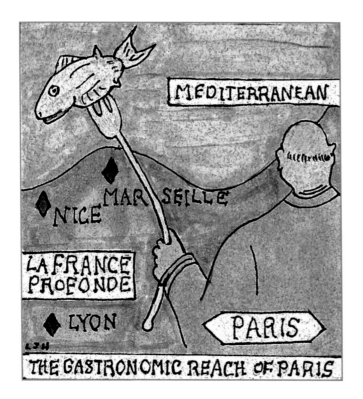

THE GASTRONOMIC REACH OF PARIS

MEDITERRANEAN

NICE — MARSEILLE

LA FRANCE PROFONDE

LYON

PARIS

In 1927, he was voted by 3,000 Parisian chefs "The Elected Prince of Gastronomy" and was the first modern food and wine critic powerful enough to make or break important restaurants. It's been claimed that many chefs would keep a table empty just in case Curnonsky should waltz in.

The hierarchy of French cuisine described in Curnonsky's books and articles includes, in descending order of refinement but not necessarily quality: haute cuisine (Paris' finest restaurants are at the top of this category); bourgeois family cooking (*la cuisine de bonne femme* or, as Curnonsky describes it, "à la

Grandma"); regional cooking where French gastronomy meets tourism; and at the bottom of the ladder, what Curnonsky calls "impromptu" or "camper" cooking, which celebrates a simple, spontaneous cuisine based on fresh, often foraged, ingredients, even road kill.

While the Paris café menu pays homage to the upper end of the gastronomic range, café food really comprises its own category with a heavy emphasis on regional specialties and iconic favorites. There is a fairly uniform menu strategy that most cafés follow (see Lessons Twelve and Thirteen on two staple café dishes, the croque monsieur and roast chicken), but many humbler cafés base their offerings on the operator's background. It turns out that café owners in Paris of yore have often come from the Auvergne region, home of the Michelin tire company and its connection to what Curnonsky called "motor tourism"—what we now call gastro-tourism. (Today it's the Chinese who are buying up Paris cafés.)

The gastronomic wheel of France in the 20th century was made of rubber. Curnonsky helped usher in the Michelin era and its starred rating system, becoming the company's first spokesman and father of touristic gastronomy. As much as Curnonsky was an haute cuisine prince, promoting regional cuisine was his real passion, and in most respects Paris café cuisine *is* regional cuisine. Much the same can be said for the American gastronome James Beard who would advocate, a generation after Curnonsky, for the regional cuisines of the United States, especially the new California cuisine that emerged in the 1970s.

It's worth noting, and rather amusing I think, the resemblance of California's revolutionary "simple, local, seasonal" cooking philosophy to Curnonsky's two lowest categories of French cuisine—regional cooking and an impromptu cooking based on foraging for ingredients, a skill that was vital to the creation of an authentic cuisine in California. Such are revolutions, political and gastronomic, that can turn traditions on their head. In California "off with his toque" became in the 1970s the gastronomical equivalent of "off with his head."

FORKS AND RAKES

Just as Paris and Berkeley "rake in" the bounty of France and California, Curnonsky and Beard did prodigious amounts of personal gastronomic raking, as their epic rotundity would testify. The French word for a rake or pitchfork is *fourche* (*foo-r*-che). A dinner fork, *fourchette* (pronounced foo-r-*shet*), is a "little rake."

The physical resemblance of our two outsized French and American gourmets goes beyond their balding pates, mustaches and signature bow ties. Like suburban sprawl around an urban core, the expansive real estate they each wore around their middles (the French call a paunch a brioche!) provided a professional trademark. As did the gluttonous Monsieur Balzac before them, the larger-than-life Curnonsky and Beard literally personified the material abundance of the foods and wines they celebrated. The pathology of their overindulgence only became a medical "problem" after World War II, especially in the U.S. When people only lived into their 30s and 40s in centuries past (especially the lower classes), obesity was not yet a disorder. But with longer life spans, thinness and dieting became a life-extending virtue, and for some an addiction and disorder (e.g., anorexia nervosa).

There is something amusing yet poignant in the discovery that at the James Beard Foundation in New York there is a long telescoping extension fork (you can purchase one online last time I checked) that Beard would use at meals to skewer (rake) food from across the table—especially bread, I am told.

HISTORICAL RAKES AND RASCALS

Appearing a century or two before Curnonsky and Beard, the "rake" was a social type that blended the dandy, rascal and libertine (the *débauché*, pronounced day-bo-*shay*) and whose large, often refined appetite was out of control, at least from the perspective of a growing conservative bourgeois culture. This character is featured in English artist William Hogarth's series of devilishly humorous paintings (and a series of lithographs based on them) called *The Rake's Progress*. The social and personal dramas portrayed in Hogarth's masterpiece reveal the troubled debauchery of one Tom Rakewell (a play on "rakehell," another word for libertine), whose "pursuit of pleasure and sensual satisfaction . . . shows hedonistic, Epicurean, and antirationalist patterns of thought" (Wikipedia).

Though the "antirationalist" component may not apply here, Curnonsky and Beard certainly shared "rakish" tendencies. Our twin gastronomes did not hesitate to pursue their "sensual satisfaction" conspicuously through their gargantuan devotions to the pleasures of the table (and privately, no doubt, through decadent behaviors not relevant to our *Café French* discourse except in a very expensive limited edition!).

MEANWHILE, BACK AT MY PARIS CAFÉ

Beard, writing about Paris' post-WWII cafés in his cookbook *Paris Cuisine*, notes that they had become home to "a very mixed crowd of phony artists, haywire poets and every possible nationality of sight-seer." Observing the scene today from the perfect flâneur's corner table at Café de Flore in Saint-Germain-des-Prés, and feeling neither particularly phony nor haywire, I wonder what Beard would think of the cafés of the 21st century and the characters (like me) who flock to them?

As for Curnonsky, whose mottos were "Good cooking is when things taste of what they are" and "Above all, keep it simple," what would he make of our post-nouvelle, hypermodernist haute cuisine cooking (aka molecular gastronomy) where first-class ingredients are transformed (and hidden) by complex alchemical technologies and theatrical presentations? What expat writer David Downie describes as "modernist daubs and swirls."

How would Curnonsky react to some ubertrendy Parisian *cuisinier de poisson* (fish cook) serving a *purée de poisson* splattered over a sheet of parchment paper and calling it "Jackson's Pollock"?

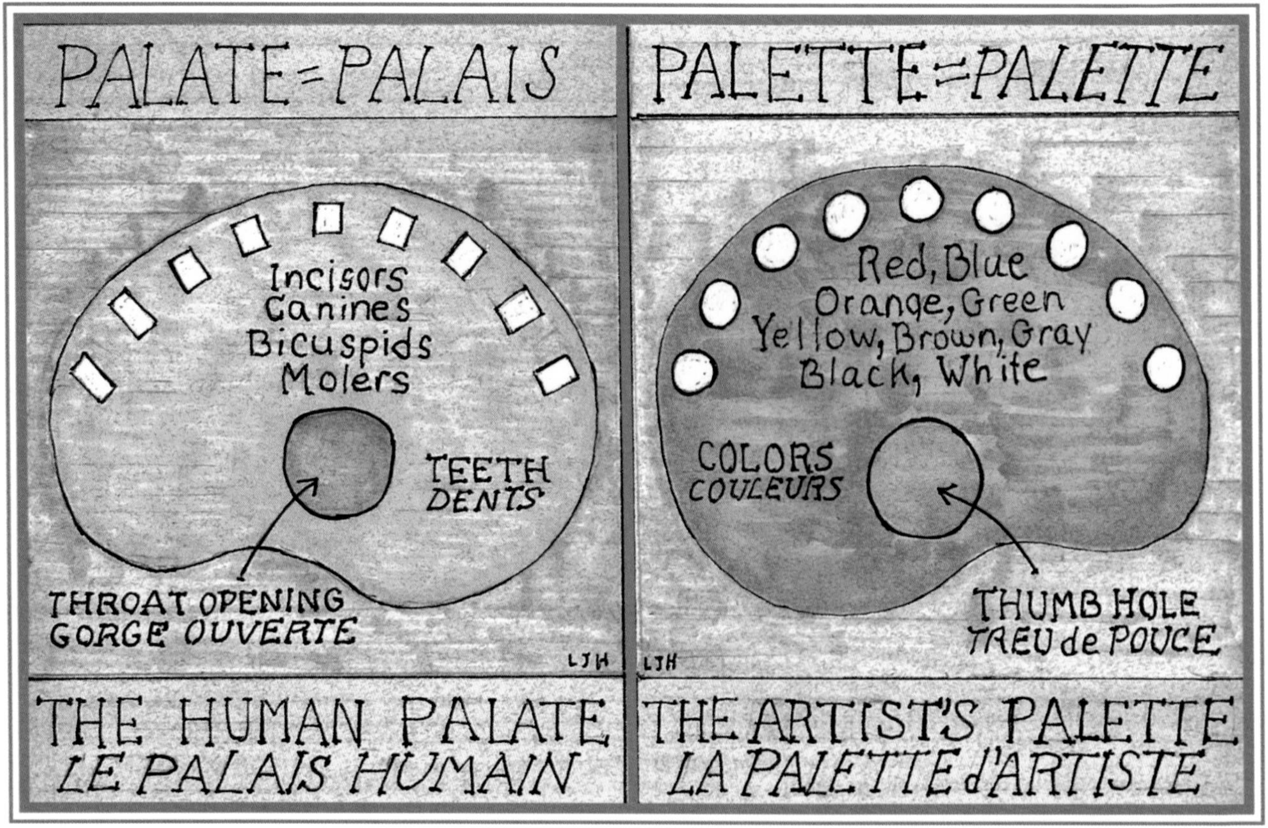
PALATE = PALAIS
Incisors
Canines
Bicuspids
Molers
TEETH
DENTS
THROAT OPENING
GORGE OUVERTE
LJH
THE HUMAN PALATE
LE PALAIS HUMAIN
PALETTE = PALETTE
Red, Blue
Orange, Green
Yellow, Brown, Gray
Black, White
COLORS
COULEURS
THUMB HOLE
TREU de POUCE
LJH
THE ARTIST'S PALETTE
LA PALETTE d'ARTISTE

Palate, Palette and Picasso's Ghostly Palace

And as soon as I recognized the taste of the piece of Madeleine soaked in her decoction of lime-blossom which my aunt used to give me . . . the whole of Combray and its surroundings, taking shape and solidity, sprang into being, town and gardens alike, from my cup of tea.

– Marcel Proust
Swann's Way

Is it merely coincidence that the artist's palette and the human palate are more than mere linguistic homophones? I was amazed, as I doodled in my journal, when their complimentary shapes emerged in my mind's eye. Perhaps it's just an artist's exaggeration. Or is it an example of pareidolia, the optical disorder where acute sufferers identify powerful images in random natural phenomena, like the image of Christ or Satan in a cloud formation or bowl of oatmeal? I think most visual artists have at least a minimal claim to this optical condition. I know I do.

I am flâneuring this morning from my apartment on boulevard Saint-Germain near rue du Bac towards the former bohemian stronghold of Montparnasse. I'm going to have lunch at Café Le Select but I'm in no hurry and stop for a crème (my second of the day) at Café de Flore, a less snooty choice than the more uppity Deux Magots just a short block away. I prefer the pretentiousness of Magots for social celebrations. Poised on the terrace in front of the Église Saint-Germain-des-Prés, the corner vantage point is magical.

At a kiosk near Flore I pick up a copy of the *International Herald Tribune*—this is before the paper was taken over by the *New York Times* in 2013. The *Herald* is a pricey guilty pleasure, but more satisfying, more international than the *Times*. I feel like Jake Barnes who, in Ernest Hemingway's *The Sun Also Rises*, sits at Flore with the Paris *Herald* and a glass of wine when he first arrives back in Paris after a visit to Spain.

On to Café Le Select. Where better to ponder the connections and distinctions between cuisine and the Fine Arts, a discussion rich with complexities linguistic, biological and aesthetic. The list of Le Select's celebrated patrons reads like a Who's Who of literary and artistic Paris in the 20s, including Ernest Hemingway, Henry Miller, Luis Buñel and Pablo Picasso. The Select may be the only café in Paris with its own biography, *Paris Café: The Select Crowd*, by Noël Riley Fitch and illustrated by gifted cartoonist Rick Tulka.

My special guests (or should I say *ghosts*?) of honor today are the gourmandizing, coffee-swilling 19th-century novelist Honoré de Balzac (see Lesson Fourteen for more on his coffee addiction) and Le Select's most celebrated alum, Picasso. We are today gastro-philologists, exploring with Balzac and Picasso both "art" and "cuisine" and the "art of cuisine."

The way I see it, the cook observes the materials arrayed on his work surface that will engage his palate (*le palais, pah*-lay) the way a painter (*le peintre, pan*-truh) views the pigments on his artist's palette (*la palette, pah*-let). The creative cook "sees" the possibilities before he even begins to chop, mix, sauté and roast.

As the cook engages with his culinary palette (the ingredients), his anatomical palate anticipates both aesthetic and gustatory taste (*le goût*, pronounced *goo*) via the interrelated physiological mechanisms of taste and smell and their influence on memory and emotion.

THE GASTRONOMY OF THE EYE

The relationship between the artist and cook, the palette and the palate, was implied by Balzac when he commented on the practice of the observing flâneur. Balzac described la flânerie as a kind of intellectual synesthesia: "the gastronomy of the eye." The artist-flâneur, like a creative cook with a pantry full of ingredients, prepares and serves his digested observations as poetry, journalism and art.

From what I know about Balzac's life, he seemed to bounce back and forth between a domestic-based workaholism and a gluttonous flânerie pursued in the finest salons, restaurants and cafés of Paris. Balzac's masterpiece, *La Comédie humaine*, is full of scenes he witnessed of the *haute bourgeoisie* feasting in the circles of high society he inhabited. (What is the connection between the decadent voyeur and the aesthetic flâneur, other than the rhyme? Food for scholarly investigation!)

THE COOK AS ARTIST

In Balzacian terms, if the observing flâneur practices the gastronomy of the eye (as in "a feast for the eyes"), the cook as artist reverses the operation, becoming the eye of gastronomy. The creative culinarian sees/tastes something we don't, like Proust remembering (seeing in his mind's eye) all of his childhood after tasting/smelling a teacake dipped into a cup of tea. The ingredients arrayed on the cook's culinary palette are transformed via aesthetic expression and registered (tasted) on the diner's palate, much as the painter's colors, poet's words or musician's notes are put together (cooked) and experienced through the relevant sense organs of the viewer, reader or listener.

This is speculative territory, though it's important to note that the French word for palate (le palais) is also the French word for palace. Bien sûr! The palate is our palace of gustatory pleasure. Before the scientific discovery in the late 19th century of taste buds (*les papilles gustatives*) distributed throughout the oral cavity, especially on the tongue, it was thought that the human palate (soft and hard) was the sole site (or seat, as in "the seat of government") of taste. Run your tongue along the roof of your mouth. It is a grand

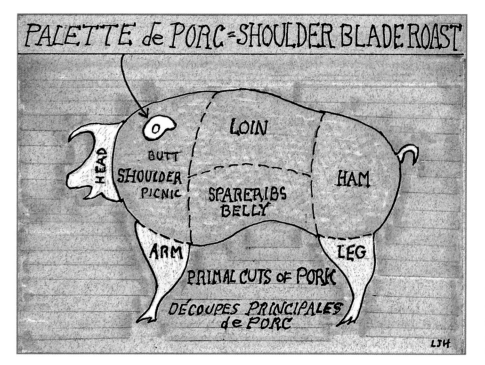

PALETTE de PORC = SHOULDER BLADE ROAST

HEAD
BUTT
SHOULDER
PICNIC
LOIN
SPARERIBS
BELLY
HAM
ARM
LEG
PRIMAL CUTS of PORK
DÉCOUPES PRINCIPALES de PORC

LJH

This part of a pig's upper shoulder is known as "Boston butt" in the U.S. and "palette" in France. It's a tough cut that needs long, slow cooking, either roasted (*rôti*) or barbecued (*cuit au barbecue*).

56

Palladian pleasure dome, no mere roof, and we with our taste-bud-studded tongues are the kings and queens of this palatial realm.

BACK AT PICASSO'S PALACE

The haunted ambiance at Le Select is palpable today. I can almost taste it. Squeezed into a cozy booth, I am reading now about the "select crowd" in Fitch's homage to the café and its historic alums. Rick Tulka's caricatures in the book bring the spirit of a bygone era to life, the history and mythology of 20th-century art and literature in Paris.

The café's resident *chat* (cat), a long-haired bohemian fellow, is asleep on the bar, adding a *je-ne-sais-quoi* (I don't know what) to the café's ambiance. Perhaps it's a *soupçon* (a touch) of domesticity, the café in its historic role as an extension of the home for the vast majority of Parisians past with their tiny apartments, even smaller (or nonexistent) kitchens, and minimal heating, lighting and plumbing.

Like penguins in their black and white garb, les garçons are scurrying about from table to table. I glance out the window at the passersby as I await my friend the food writer, cookbook author and French pastry expert Martha Rose Shulman, who will be joining me today.

I have important questions for Martha—about Picasso, not *pâtisserie*—who spent the 1980s living in Paris and operating her home-based Supper Club chez Martha Rose. She grew close (and still is) to her landlord, Christine, who she soon discovered was the widow of Pablo Picasso's late son Paulo Picasso. Martha is my closest connection to the real, historic Picasso—Picasso outside the myth.

I've read a lot about the palette of Picasso, but I know little of his palate. Señor Picasso was an Andalusian. I presume that he loved garlic, peppers and grilled sardines, a specialty of his native Málaga. It has been reported in the press that his Provençal favorites were eel stew made with lots of garlic, and a Niçoise omelette made tortilla-style (like a pancake). Martha knows more but will speak only off the record, as she has in previous conversations, in order to protect the privacy of Christine. We will sit on Le Select's terrace and, like good gastro-flâneurs, observe the action on boulevard du Montparnasse and the action on our plates: salade niçoise, croque monsieur and afterwards *un dessert* with a café noir or crème. I will drink in Martha's stories about Paris and Picasso, and the café's nosy and noisy ghosts will be all atwitter.

Piecasso.

I've always wondered about Picasso's self-portrait of 1906. What was he holding in his right hand? One would assume a paintbrush given that in his left hand is a palette. Or perhaps the palette had been in his right hand and he made the change. To my eye the portrait has always seemed unfinished, but in Picasso's case, that would be an irrelevant consideration. I don't remember what caused me to place a pie into the image and then reconstruct his signature as "Piecasso." This was in 2008 when I was transitioning from collage work to my "foodoodle" cartoons.

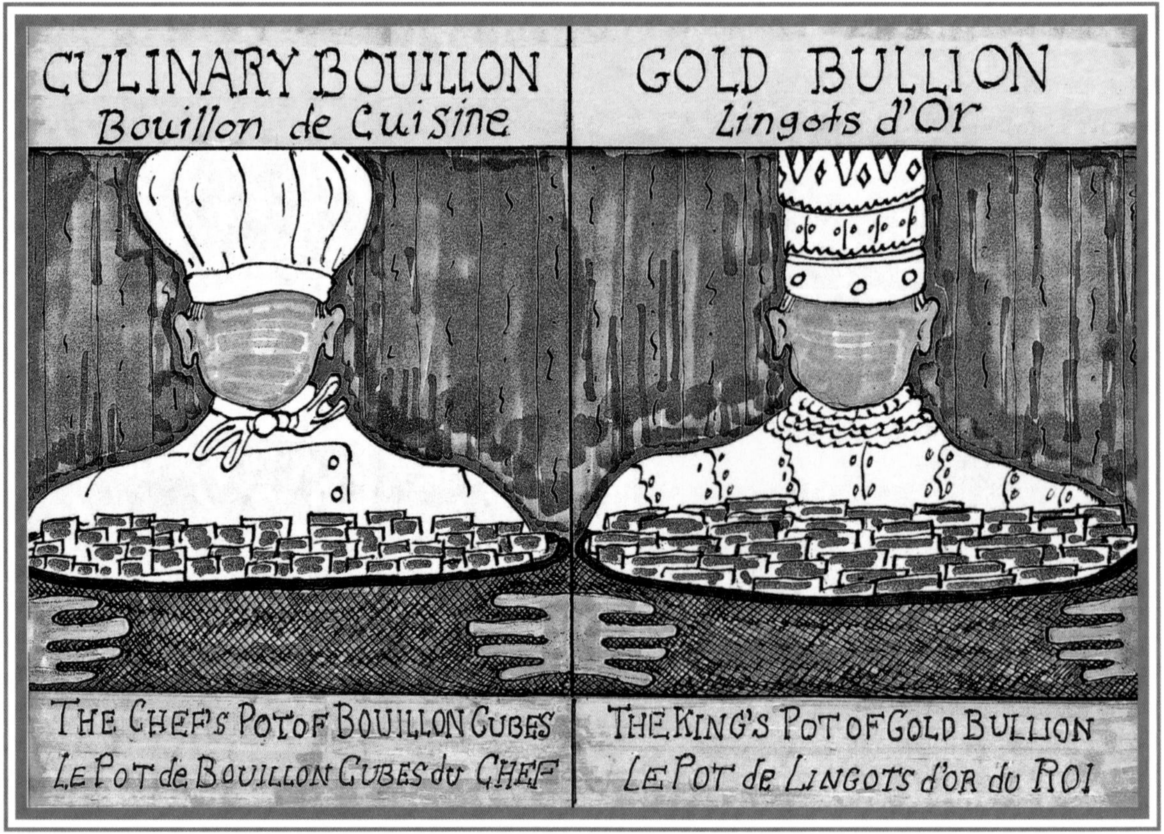
CULINARY BOUILLON
Bouillon de Cuisine
GOLD BULLION
Lingots d'Or
THE CHEF'S POT OF BOUILLON CUBES
LE POT de BOUILLON CUBES du CHEF
THE KING'S POT OF GOLD BULLION
LE POT de LINGOTS d'OR du ROI

BOUILLON MEETS BULLION IN A SOUP POT

I will not wear a crown of gold where my savior wore one of thorns.

– Godfrey of Bouillon
First King of Jerusalem

Bouillon Chartier, which opened on rue du Faubourg Montmartre in 1896, is not exactly a café or bistro or brasserie, though it serves as all three. Chartier is, in fact, a *bouillon* (*boo*-yon, pronounced with a soft, nasal "n"), one of a few surviving members of a class of Parisian restaurants of the mid-to-late 19th century that specialized in hearty fare—especially meaty, "restorative" soups and broths. Sort of like a soup kitchen without the charitable angle. The low prices at les bouillons attracted workers, artists and shopkeepers in and around the sprawling food markets of Les Halles during the period of rapid commercial expansion in Paris during the Second Empire.

Credit for the creation of the bouillon goes to Pierre-Louis Duval, an enterprising butcher whose first "broth Duval" opened in 1855. By 1900, the year of the Universal Exposition in Paris, there were hundreds of bouillons in Belle Époque Paris, some fancier than Duval's originals (Art Nouveau interiors were the rage), catering now to the increasingly affluent bourgeoisie.

PRIMORDIAL SOUP

It's well documented that the modern restaurant (the word and the place) evolved from the restorative meat broths (called *restaurants*, pronounced res-toe-*ron*) served at "health food" establishments in Paris beginning in the late 18th century. These early restaurants were operated by chefs cast off from their kitchens in the homes of aristocrats who had fled or died (*la guillotine*) during the French Revolution.

Going back still further to the 15th century, a very interesting recipe for a "restaurant" is documented in Rebecca Spang's fascinating book *The Invention of the Restaurant: Paris and Modern Gastronomic Culture*. The recipe is from French master chef Chiquart Amiczo in his cookery book, *Du fait de cuysine* (1420). Amiczo's instructions, according to Spang, call for cooking a freshly killed chicken in an alchemist's glass kettle along with sixty gold ducats. Amiczo writes that other precious stones are usable if a doctor so orders. Not exactly the recipe my grandmother used when she made her famously golden chicken soup to cure my colds.

COURTING THE GOLDEN BOUILLON

Let us explicate the linguistic trajectory between bouillon/broth (nourishment) and bullion/gold (commerce)—that is, between *restaurants* (an Old French word for restorative broths) and restaurants (dining establishments in both French and English).

The English pronunciation of the French "bouillon," with a hard "n" (*yone*) is the same as for the English word "bullion." Bullion, uncoined gold (or silver) in the form of bars (ingots in English and *lingots* in French), derives from the Old French *billion*, a bar of precious metal, and *bille*, a wood block or stick. According to etymological accounts, both bouillon and bullion derive from the Latin *bullire* (to boil or make bubbles).

The Anglo-French word "billion" has confusing origins because, although derived from the Old French *billion* and an older version, *byllion*, in British English the word billion has meant bi-million or million million (trillion) until recent times. The French and other European languages adopted another word for billion, *milliard* (a thousand million), to avoid the confusion between the so-called "long scale" and "short scale" forms of counting large numbers in academic circles. Confusing indeed!

To make gold bullion one has to "boil" the gold to liquefy it for the ingot molds. Here is the recipe for a golden "quick bouillon" (the French *court-bouillon*, pronounced *coor*-boo-yon), the vegetable-based broth used for poaching fish and light meats: boil carrots, celery, onion, parsley, bay leaf, thyme and lemon in water, adding white wine or vinegar. Gold ducats to taste.

Or cheat and avoid culinary/alchemical complexity by using dehydrated bouillon cubes, such as organic ibo-brand *bouillon de poule en cubes*. Just add boiling water (*l'eau bouillante*).

FOLLOW THE MONNAIE

The pot thickens! Let's look at a small slice of French history that is as startling as it is inconsequential, the almost simultaneous arrival of two men to the court of King Louis XIII (son of Henry IV) in the first half of the 17th century, one named Bullion and the other Bouillon. (I did not, indeed could not, make this up.)

Claude de Bullion was a French aristocrat who served as Minster of Finance under Louis XIII from 1632 to 1640. He is credited with the creation of the Louis d'Or gold coin, which replaced the Spanish doubloon, coined money (*monnaie*, pronounced *mon*-et, as in, "A Monet costs *beaucoup de monnaie*") then in circulation in France. At least one source insists that the origin of the word "bullion" derives from Lord Bullion's name, but can this be true given the word's etymological connection to Old French and Latin cognates?

The other man, Henri de la Tour d'Auvergne, the Duc de Bouillon, was born in 1555 into the royal line associated with the Duchy of Bouillon in northeastern France, which later became incorporated into Belgium. An earlier Lord of Bouillon, Godfrey of Bouillon (Godefroy de Bouillon, 1060–1100), was a Frankish knight who was one of the leaders of the First Crusade. When the Crusade ended in 1099, Bouillon became the first ruler of the Kingdom of Jerusalem.

Today the Belgian city of Bouillon attracts tourists to its medieval castle, Château de Bouillon. Louis XIII was still a boy in 1610 when the Duc de Bouillon became a member of the Council of Regency and a favorite of the Queen Regent Marie de Médicis. I have found no evidence that Bullion and Bouillon knew each other, but it's interesting to speculate about what might have happened if Monsieur Gold and Monsieur Broth had met each other. Stock (shares/broth) may have changed hands/mouths quicker than you can say "liquid investment"!

Godfrey of Bouillon: A modest fellow, this Lord of Bouillon preferred the title Advocate of the Holy Sepulchre to King of Jerusalem. Christ, he claimed, was the only King of Jerusalem. This portrait is based on a fresco painted by Giacomo Jaquerio in Saluzzo (northern Italy) around 1420.

TAKING STOCK AT CHARTIER

Seated at a small table at Chartier, I find no bouillon on the menu—no soup, potage or consommé of any kind at the Paris home of soup. *Sacrebleu* (OMG)! My garçon explains that the weather is too hot for soup. Imagine a Parisian café on a hot day with no café!

Despite my disappointment, I can taste the history of Parisian broth in Chartier's authentic Belle Époque interior. I feel as if I have traveled back in time to the Paris of Emile Zola's *The Belly of Paris*, his novel set in Les Halles and the charcuteries, bistros, cafés and bouillons of the Second Empire. A bit of time regained.

During that extraordinary period, Pierre-Louis Duval's chain of bouillons had made him a "bouillonaire." But his son, Alexandre—according to fellow Berkeley writer and Francophile Susan Griffin, author of *The Book of the Courtesans: A Catalogue of Their Virtues*—squandered much of the family's wealth on the notorious and exquisite courtesan Cora Pearl.

When Pearl dumped the young, naive Duval, he tried to shoot her with a pistol that misfired. As a result, he almost took his own life. The scandal that rocked *tout Paris* tilted in favor of the scorned Duval and brought down Pearl, who fled to London—the land of Dickens and tea—where she was born. The "affaire Duval" (some 20 years before l'Affaire Dreyfus) was a wake-up call for the bouillon heir who recovered and rebuilt the broth empire he inherited.

Along with Art Nouveau and the Belle Époch, the golden age of Parisian bouillons and courtesans is past. The fabled Bouillon Chartier is a somewhat sad and semi-soupless shadow of its former self. (There is now a second Chartier location in Montparnasse and reports are that the food is better than at the original.) Luckily for the institution of the Parisian café, the thirst for hot coffee—a universal, all-weather restorative brew—will never dry up. Nor, hopefully, will the historically rich Bouillon Chartier, with or without bouillon.

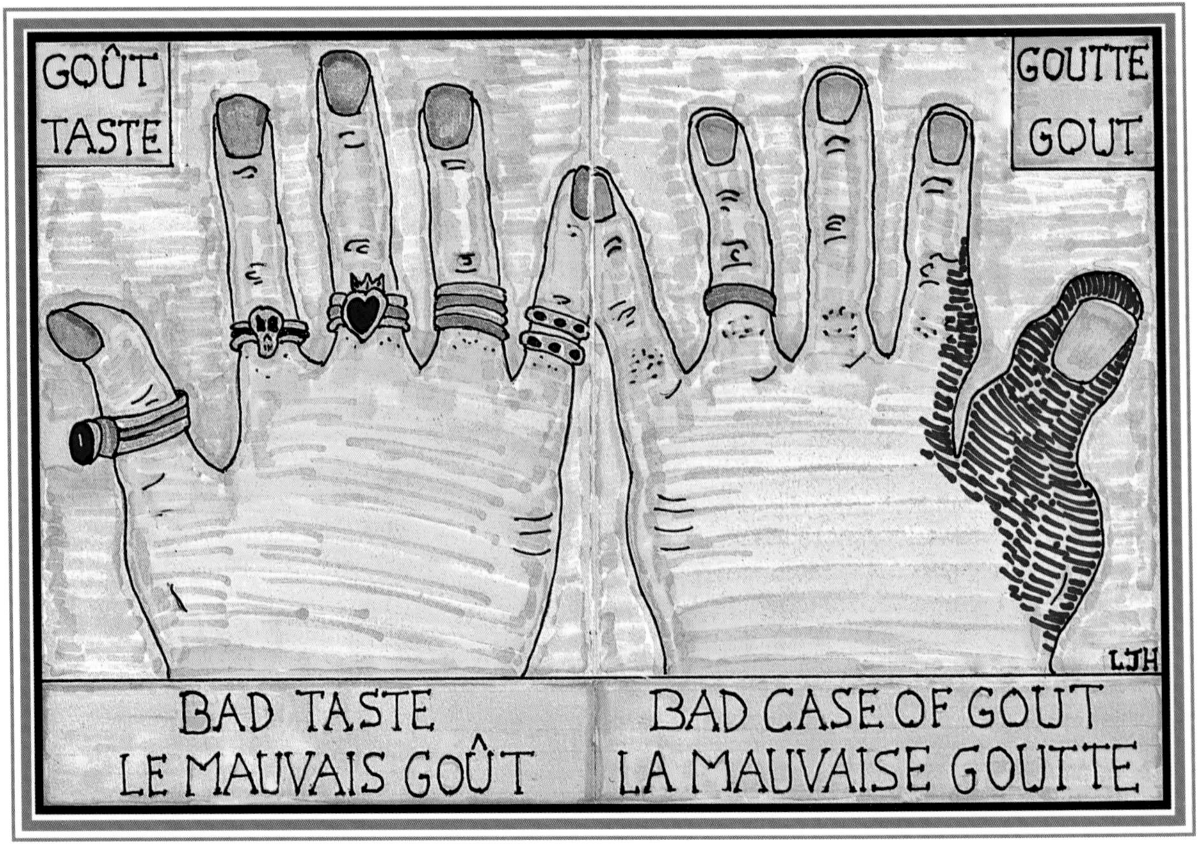
GOÛT
TASTE
GOUTTE
GOUT
LJH
BAD TASTE
LE MAUVAIS GOÛT
BAD CASE OF GOUT
LA MAUVAISE GOUTTE

Uncle Wiggily, Voltaire and le Bon Goût

Language is a very difficult thing to put into words.

–Voltaire

I remember an important lesson with gastronomic implications from a book of children's bedtime stories. I loved this classic series by Howard R. Garis featuring the rheumatic Uncle Wiggily Longears, an elderly, kind and very wise rabbit. In each illustrated story, Uncle Wiggily confronts the vagaries of life in his woodland habitat and solves a problem or fends off a threat within his community of furry critters and the children who know them.

The one episode I recall best is about a young squirrel or possum with a taste for candy that gets a terrible tummy ache from overindulging. Uncle Wiggily comes to the rescue and I vividly remember the moral of the story, a classic Wiggliy maxim: "Too much of anything is not too good!" A maxim that, I confess, I have not always abided by, especially when in Paris where it's almost impossible to curb culinary enthusiasms.

Uncle Wiggily's lesson in hunger management is a Hallmark card version of Mark Twain's earlier and more humorous quip, "Too much of anything is bad, but too much good whiskey is barely enough." Truth be told, despite wise Wiggily's input into my early childhood development, Twain's version comes much closer to "the gastronomical me," to borrow the title from the great American writer M. F. K. Fisher's culinary memoir. Paraphrasing Twain, "Too much of anything is bad, but too much good *food* is barely enough."

Which brings me circuitously to some curious semantic connections between biological (sensory) and aesthetic (intellectual) taste (*goût*) and the ailment gout (*goutte*, pronounced *goot*), caused by, one might say, too much goût for rich food and alcohol.

IT'S ALL GREEK, LATIN, OLD FRENCH AND ANGLO-SAXON TO ME

In both English and French, the use of the same words—taste in English and gôut in French—for both general aesthetic appreciation *and* perception of flavor appears to be deeply embedded in our two languages and yet confoundedly convoluted. As the French Enlightenment thinker and Café Le Procope regular Voltaire (1694–1788) explained in his *Philosophical Dictionary*, the English language "is a copy of ours in almost all the words which are not Saxon." The etymological links between French goût and English taste, and between French goutte (gout) and English gout are no mere accident and took centuries to develop.

Here is a glossary that attempts to connect the dots using a variety of etymological sources, though I am no Denis Diderot, the great Enlightenment encyclopedist and another Procope habitué:

Goût *(FR):* From the Latin *gustus* and *gutta*, and Old French *goust* = **Taste**
  "Gustatory" in English and gustatif in French come from the same root. By the 18th century in France, goût was associated with aesthetic taste.

Goutte *(FR):* From the Latin *gutta* and Old French *gote* = **Gout and Drop**
  It was thought as far back as the 9th century that this inflammatory ailment was caused by little drops of viscous humors seeping from the blood into the joints causing painful swelling, a theory close to the modern explanation. The Latin gutta also gives us the English "gutter," which we will visit in Lesson Eleven in our discussion of the gargoyle's practical function as a rain gutter for Gothic churches.

Gout *(ENG):* Derives from the Old French *gote* = **Goutte**

> Note Voltaire's comment above about the French origin of many non-Saxon (Germanic) English words.

Taste *(ENG):* From the Vulgar Latin *tastare* and Old French *tast* (touch) = **Goût**

> The Old English *smaec* (to taste) derives from the German *schmecken*, which translates as "to taste, try, smell, and perceive." Hence taste, with its Old French connection to "touch," has a more assertive (hands-on) connotation than the passive Old English/Germanic cognates smaecken/schmecken, which can be translated as "sensibility."

But why the same words in English and French for both aesthetic and physical taste? I have not found an acceptable answer for why our sense of taste/gôut—the human faculty *least* associated with art with a capital A (the Fine Arts)—is used as the term for discerning, as Voltaire put it, "the feeling of beauty and defects in all the arts."

The 20th-century philologist Carl Darling Buck states in his authoritative *A Dictionary of Selected Synonyms in the Principal Indo-European Languages* (1949) that "Of all the five senses, 'taste' is the one most closely associated with fine discrimination, hence the familiar secondary uses of words for 'taste, good taste' with reference to aesthetic discrimination."

But the question is not answered: *Why?* In her essay "Playing to the Senses: Food as a Performance Medium," scholar Barbara Kirshenblatt-Gimblett comes closer:

> *While taste as an aesthetic faculty lacks a dedicated organ, Enlightenment aesthetics thought of it as "le sens interne du beau" or the sixth sense within us, whose organs we cannot see.*

OK, then, *two* organs for discerning gôut, one visible and one invisible. That's one way to resolve this conundrum. After taste (tongue) and smell (nose), the other Aristotelian sense organs (note the musical context of the word "organ") are used in organ-specific contexts to describe aesthetic taste. For example, you can have an eye for design and an ear for music. But you can't have an eye for music or an ear for sculpture. The inner sixth organ that applies universally to all the arts just needs a name. It has been called intuition but that doesn't quite work for me either.

My own view would be that taste/goût applies to all the arts because when we taste something we not only touch it (oral contact), we bring it *into* the body itself which renders taste unique and more "intimate" than the other senses. Kirshenblatt-Gimblett notes, "Voltaire wrote that 'Taste is not content with seeing, with knowing the beauty of a work; it has to feel it, to be touched by it.' " This tactile dimension of goût is crucial. After all, tasting "bad" food can kill you. Bad art just makes you sick.

The other utilitarian art form that can kill you is architecture, with its faulty structures, poisonous materials, etc. Yet architecture is included in the traditional Fine Arts pantheon, while cuisine earns (almost begrudgingly, it seems to me) the status of "the Culinary Arts," at best a subset of the Fine Arts. Why? Perhaps because, unlike cuisine, which is ephemeral (consumed), architecture and the other visual arts persist over time as objects. They can be recorded photographically. The nonvisual fine arts too can be recorded (i.e., reexperienced) via sound recording (music), video recording (dance, theater, performance art) and print (literature).

TASTE, MEMORY AND TASTE MEMORY

The primary aesthetic dimension of a meal, the nonvisual experience of its goût, cannot be recorded except in memory and in written form as a recipe. Hence the term of art that food professionals love to use, "taste memory," a talent many chefs and food writers possess for remembering a dish or a flavor. This memory can be used to "reproduce" the dish in the kitchen, but it's not the original. It's not the same taste, the same dish, the same experience.

Modern science explains the link between taste (and more so the sense of smell, as 80% of our taste is actually smell) and memory as a hardwired link between the brain's olfactory bulb and the "old" or mammalian brain (the limbic system), which sits below the neocortex, or new brain. Marcel Proust's *In Search of Lost Time*, based on taste memories triggered in the novel's narrator by the smell of a tiny Madeleine cake dipped into an herbal tea, is one of the most profound expressions in literature of the powerful and mysterious nature of human goût and its relationship to memory.

It must be noted that although a taste/smell of tea triggered Proust's access to his childhood memories,

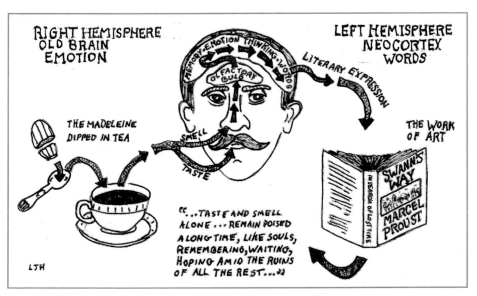

RIGHT HEMISPHERE
OLD BRAIN
EMOTION

LEFT HEMISPHERE
NEOCORTEX
WORDS

MEMORY • EMOTION   THINKING • WORDS

LITERARY EXPRESSION

OLFACTORY BULB

THE MADELEINE
DIPPED IN TEA

SMELL

TASTE

THE WORK
OF ART

SWANN'S WAY

IN SEARCH OF LOST TIME

MARCEL PROUST

"...TASTE AND SMELL
ALONE... REMAIN POISED
A LONG TIME, LIKE SOULS,
REMEMBERING, WAITING,
HOPING AMID THE RUINS
OF ALL THE REST..."

LJH

Proust's Way: Although controversial, left brain/right brain theory gives us something to work with when we try to understand the relationship between emotion/memory and taste/smell (a right brain function) and how this is translated into language (a left brain function). The drawing presents a very simplified map of Marcel Proust's transformation of taste memory into prose.

it was high doses of caffeine from multiple daily cups of *café au lait*, delivered to him in his sick bed by his housekeeper/assistant, Céleste, that helped the dying Proust finish his seven-volume novel.

VOLTAIRE AND NAPOLEON AT LE PROCOPE

Voltaire's ideas about taste were formed during the Enlightenment. France was just beginning its reign as Europe's capital of *le bon goût* in art, style, fashion and gastronomy, in the wake of the patronage and appetites—shoes, perfume, gilded furniture, luxurious fabrics—of the Sun King, Louis XIV (1638–1715). I think of Louis XIV as the Ralph Lauren of French monarchs. He must also be credited for his relatively liberal policies related to the new cafés and their function as safe spaces for the expression of radical ideas. Agents of the court (police) were sent to cafés more to spy on suspicious characters than to arrest them.

By the early 1700s, the Paris café had arrived as the chic nexus of good taste (both kinds) and the go-to spot for the new, exotic beverage—coffee—and another trendy draw introduced by Le Procope's Sicilian owner, Francesco Procopio: lemon ice (sorbet). While well-caffeinated literary men inside Le Procope debated the latest plays performed across the street at the Comédie-Française, fashionable ladies could be found parked outside in their carriages, procuring cups of sorbet. But more than in any other European capital, according to Joan DeJean in *The Essence of Style: How the French Invented High Fashion, Fine Food, Chic Cafés, Style, Sophistication, and Glamour*, elegant women were also welcome *inside* the chic Paris cafés of the day.

Cafés in those days catered to a small Parisian elite. "Taste, like philosophy," Voltaire noted, "belongs only to a small number of privileged souls." But as France headed into revolutionary mode at the end of the 18th century, the Parisian cafés' clientele broadened to include poets and artists, radical politicians and one young military officer in particular—Napoleon Bonaparte. Napoleon spent time in the cafés of the Palais Royal on the Right Bank, but also at Le Procope in the Latin Quarter. History records that on one occasion, when he forgot to bring his purse, the future Emperor was forced to leave his signature bicorne hat as a pledge until he could return with payment. There is a glass-enclosed display vitrine at Le Procope today, right at the entrance, that holds a dusty old and very tiny bicorne attributed to Bonaparte. If authentic, Napoleon's very large ambition was parked inside a very small skull. But it's hard to imagine that it is

July 6 '90

Boeuf Wellington vs Napoleon

Either the Duke of W. loved this dish: fillet coated w/ pâté de foie gras and duxelles then wrapped in puff pastry or any version of filet de Boeuf en croute or that the dish looked like boots worn by Wellington. "Brown shiny boots." Origins not clear. Italian origin—"Napoleon": puff paste.

FRANCE   ENGLAND

an Napoleon   vs   an Boeuf Wellington

Napoleon vs. Wellington: This quick sketch from my journal shows a battlefield meet-up between Napoleon and Wellington at Waterloo. Napoleon surrendered to Wellington there, but in my version of history, Bonaparte presents to Wellington a plated "Napoleon" while Wellington offers up his "Beef Wellington" which, as with the Napoleon, has nothing to do with him. The overly heavy, stuffed and rolled English beef dish *en croute* (in a pastry crust) became identified with Wellington because it was thought, according to some food (not foot) historians, to resemble the shape of his long, cylindrical boot. In fact, the Wellington-designed boot may have, as much as anything else, beat Napoleon on the battlefield, as French soldiers were marching and fighting with inferior footwear. In my sketchy gastronimized Waterloo, Napoleon ultimately defeats Wellington, just as the adored culinary Napoleon has won out over the almost-forgotten Beef Wellington. In any case, and regardless of the dish's virtues when done right, who wants to eat something that looks like an old boot?

anything other than an aged facsimile. Au contraire says the café's manager, who asserts in a TV interview that it's the real thing. He quips at the end, "We are still waiting for him."

The vitrine, the commemorative plaques devoted to celebrity regulars—among whom Denis Diderot, Jean-Jacques Rousseau, Benjamin Franklin and Paul Verlaine, in addition to Voltaire and Napoleon—the elegant 18th-century-style furnishings: all this weaves a spell that renders Le Procope's underwhelming classic French brasserie food a delight.

On the dessert menu at Le Procope is, of course, the classic French *mille-feuille*, a confection known in the U.S. and other countries as the Napoleon. Not so in France. It turns out that the rich, flaky dessert made from thin pastry sheets (*feuille* means leaf) layered with pastry cream has more to do with an older Italian treat from Naples (Napoli). The French have refused to adopt the name "Napoleon."

Arthur Wellesley
Duke of Wellington

> Hats off to the iconic "Napoleon," but my masterpiece, "Beef Wellington," is a brilliant assemblage of succulent beef tenderloin coated with rich liver pate and mushroom duxelles, then wrapped in puff pastry and baked to a golden brown. A true classic in the pantheon of Western gastronomy.

Napoleon Bonaparte
Emperor of France

> Yes, Waterloo was Wellington's win, but gastronomy is mine! His beef dish has all the flavor, and appearance, of an old leather boot. My dessert, the "Napoleon," made from ineffably thin leaves of crisp pastry layered with butter cream, is the French confection par excellence.

LJH

I got a bit obsessed with this comparative analysis of the Napoleon versus Beef Wellington. In 2014 I drew portraits of the two iconic warriors and created narratives for their respective culinary positions. I even built a museum-style vitrine to display facsimiles of Napoleon's bicorne hat and Wellington's boot along with narrative bubbles, museum-style labels and the portraits. It's mounted in my library in Berkeley.

UNCLE WIGGILY VISITS PARIS

Today, Le Procope serves its history and bon goût to an even broader swath of souls who are less privileged than in Voltaire's day, less political than in Napoleon's, less poetic than in Verlaine's, but no less human. Tourists.

Imagine now a further democratization of the Parisian café in our age of animal rights expressed in a new chapter in Uncle Wiggily's adventures. The elderly gentleman rabbit, dressed in his dandiest duds, ventures out of the forest to flâner in Paris with a tour group of young furry souls: chipmunks, possums, muskrats and bear cubs. They are seated at Voltaire's favorite table at Le Procope where they furiously nibble away on tiny wedges of quiche and mini mille-feuille pastries, washed down with ravenous little gulps of *chocolat chaud*, the drink that Voltaire popularized at Le Procope (i.e., coffee with enough chocolate to round out its sharp edges). Uncle Wiggily Longears, alarmed by this spectacle of gluttonous bon goût, once again warns his charges, this time in his best bunny French, *"Trop de bonnes choses n'est pas bon!"* Too much of anything is not too good!

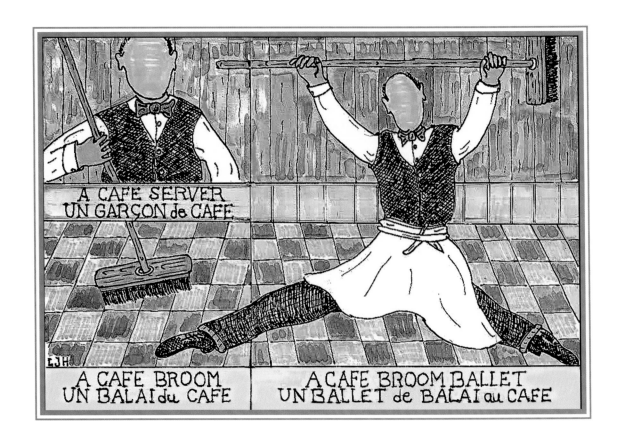

A CAFE SERVER
UN GARÇON de CAFE

A CAFE BROOM
UN BALAI du CAFE

A CAFE BROOM BALLET
UN BALLET de BALAI au CAFE

Of Brooms and Ennui on Île Saint-Louis

There is nothing so insupportable to man as to be in entire repose, without passion, occupation, amusement, or application. Then it is that he feels his own nothingness, isolation, insignificance, dependent nature, powerlessness, emptiness. Immediately there issue from his soul ennui, sadness, chagrin, vexation, despair.

– Blaise Pascal

Île Saint-Louis, one of two small islands floating in the middle of the river Seine and hyped in travel literature as "a peaceful oasis of calm" in the heart of busy Paris, is anything but, especially during the summer. A tourist Mecca, bien sûr, filled with snazzy shops, restaurants and cafés, and home to the legendary Berthillon ice cream. The scene is more Coney Island fun park than Parisian island oasis.

I'm sitting in the island's trendiest café, Café Saint-Régis on rue Jean du Bellay, just across the Pont Saint-Louis bridge connecting Paris' other natural island, Île de la Cité, where Notre Dame resides in all its gloomy Gothic glamour. The Café Saint-Régis is what I would call *faux belle*, refurbished to evoke the gaudy Art Deco atmosphere of Belle Époque Paris, with gaudy prices to match. Like the island itself, the café feels cloying.

LIVING IN A PARISIAN BROOM CLOSET

Whatever joie de vivre Parisian cafés evoke, I'm not buying it today at the Saint-Régis. As noted in Lesson Three, cafés have their dark, existential side. Throughout history, revolutions and assassinations have been plotted, even launched in Parisian cafés. Suicides too. But my dark mood today is more ennui—that nuanced French word for boredom laced with melancholy—than suicidal depression. Why would I be depressed, a magazine writer on a summer assignment in chic central Paris?

But the apartment I'm staying in on Île Saint-Louis is painfully smaller than the rental agency photos indicated. So I vegetate (call it work if you like) in the island's cafés, upscale and down, to escape domestic claustrophobia, something apartment-dwelling Parisians—and there are virtually no other kind—have been doing for centuries.

The only hint of joie at the Saint-Régis today is triggered by a garçon waltzing (literally) around the café with his broom—a Parisian push broom, a smaller version of the type of broom we use in the U.S. for exterior clean-ups. I could write a whole treatise on France's bizarre broom methodology: In short, Parisians push, they don't sweep.

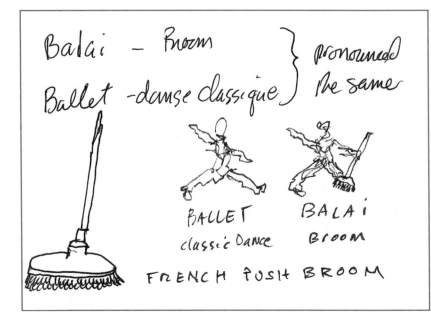

Balai — Broom
Ballet -danse classique } pronounced the same

BALLET
classic Dance

BALAI
Broom

FRENCH PUSH BROOM

At Café Saint-Régis I sketched my garçon waltzing around the café with a push broom. I had not known the French word for broom—*balai*—or its *faux amis* relationship with ballet in both English and French.

Googling broom history and its etymology in both French and English, I come across—*par hasard* (by chance)—this lesson's Anglo-French homophones: *le ballet* (the dance) and *le balai* (broom), identically pronounced: *bal*-ai. Ah ha! My server, dressed in formal café black and white, is executing *un ballet de balai*—a broom ballet. A broom ballet on rue Jean du Bellay. Ennui morphs into *bonheur* (happiness).

A WHOLE LOTTA LOUIS GOIN' ON

Back at the apartment my mood darkens. Inexplicably, the sight of a push broom leaning against the kitchen wall triggers gloom's return. Maybe it's a case of island fever; or the pall of overcast skies; or the palpable weight of French history that hovers over the island like a monstrous gold crown dripping with jewels.

Everywhere you stroll on Île Saint-Louis there are references to King Louis IX, France's beloved Saint Louis and the island's namesake. Bridges, streets, hotels, churches and cafés carry the name or variants. Even the word *régis* in Café Saint-Régis, means "of the king" in Latin. My modest corner café/brasserie where I go for my morning petit déjeuner is named Le Louis IX. It was Louis XIII in the 17th century, dubbed "the Just," who developed the island's urban plan—it had been a cow pasture. And it was he who named the island in honor of Saint Louis.

À propos of royal sobriquets, I discover that several of the eighteen French King Louis have earned less than flattering nicknames. In the 9th century there was "the Stammerer" (Louis II), in the 10th "the Lazy" (Louis V) and in the 12th "the Fat" (Louis VI). You could say that the French have had a love/hate relationship with their mostly House of Bourbon Louis. Honestly, I'm surprised there was never a "Shrimp Louis." The likely candidate would be King Louis XVII, son of guillotined King Louis XVI and Marie Antoinette. Never attaining the throne after the revolution, the Dauphin died in prison at age ten. He didn't live long enough to earn a snappy moniker. Now he has one, no charge.

"THE BEHEADED" | "SHRIMP LOUIS"

KING LOUIS XVI
1754-1793

KING LOUIS XVII
1785-1795

After his father's execution and older brother's death, the young Louis-Charles (1785-1795) became the next in line for the crown—Louis XVII. Though the boy died at age ten, his body was never formally identified and a legend has persisted that he escaped his imprisonment. Finally, in 2000, DNA testing on his remains proved that the "lost Dauphine" had indeed died in 1795, presumably from tuberculosis.

SPEAKING OF SALADS

If I thought my one-bedroom apartment was small, I was corrected at dinner in the *chambre de bonne* (maid's quarters) of the Paris guidebook author Annabel Simms, an English expat. Her book *An Hour from Paris* is a perennial seller in Paris and is designed to take tourists out of crowded Paris for memorable day trips.

The fifth-floor studio walk-up on the island's main drag, rue Saint-Louis-en-l'Île (of course), is equipped with a tiny wall-mounted kitchenette: two burners with fridge and sink tucked under the counter. "And," Simms boasts, "no microwave!"

Petite with short, dirty-blonde hair, Simms, a friend of a friend, tells me that she is working on a recipe book geared to simple French apartment cooking. She serves her version of Elizabeth David's Salade Parisienne from *French Provincial Cooking*, composed of fresh vegetables, hard-boiled egg and slices of room-temperature roast beef (which Simms purchased cooked from a local shop) all dressed with a vibrant (leaning to the acidic) vinaigrette. Simply delicious, and perfect for the warm summer night.

Over coffee our conversation drifts towards my host's mixed reviews of her island oasis lifestyle. Simms has been living frugally and productively, and I assume happily, on the pricey Île Saint-Louis for more than twenty years. She avoids expensive touristy spots like Café Saint-Régis. "I love their baby Spanish sardines served in the tin with the lid rolled up," she confesses, "but I'd rather go to the cheaper Café Le Lutèce next door with its terrace facing north towards the Seine and the quieter Right Bank."

The next day, back for a farewell crème at Café Saint-Régis before returning to the States, I ponder Simms' somewhat cloistered life on the island. It's ironic that over the course of her decades here, she has built her career as a writer in Paris, a city she obviously adores, based on a book that encourages tourists to get *out* of Paris. After three weeks sequestered on Île Saint-Louis, I'm ready to get out too.

Note the initials "JSC" in the right corner of the image. They stand for *Je suis Charlie*, a slogan that became popular after the killings in 2015 at the *Charlie Hebdo* magazine headquarters in Paris. Cartoonists, musicians and writers were using the slogan as a sign of solidarity with the satirical magazine and the universal principles of free speech. I was finishing this drawing at that time. I put JSC—suggesting also Jesus Christ—in the panel with the crucified rabbit. More satire/blasphemy.

Bread, Pain and Chocolate Rabbits

There is a communion of more than our bodies when bread is broken and wine drunk.

– M. F. K. Fisher

Bread and pain. The staff of life and the pain of life. One could hardly imagine more disparate phenomena. Nevertheless, the French word for bread is *pain*. Given no discernable etymological link between the French *pain* and the English "pain," it would appear that what is at play here is some random *frisson de langue*. With a common alphabet of only twenty-six letters there are bound to be some odd bedfellows in English and French, *n'est-ce pas*?

Let's explore these faux amis a little further. I am back again in Oakland, California, in the vibrant Rockridge district where I will be joined for breakfast and a French lesson at Oliveto Café by Lisa Taylor, a Paris-born linguist and French teacher. She'll be able to shed some light on our subject, *sans aucun doute* (without a doubt).

Oliveto leans heavily to the Italian in their upstairs white-tablecloth restaurant but the café, with its indoor/outdoor terraces, is one of the few in the East Bay that reminds me of my favorite cafés in Paris. The clientele is somewhat older and better dressed than at any café I know of around these parts. There are even patrons wearing scarves and servers wearing black! A grand spot to ponder the semantic nuances of bread and pain.

BREAKING BREAD IS A PAIN

Ms. Taylor arrives in an outfit that screams "Paris"—shiny skin-tight pants, a beautiful floral blouse, a skimpy leather jacket and, of course, an artfully arranged scarf. You can take the linguist out of Paris. . . "Bonjour, Jean," she says, setting the stage for my painful efforts at speaking French. "Bonjour, Mademoiselle," I say, warming up my linguistic muscles.

After settling in and ordering—poached eggs and a latte for me; smoked salmon, cream cheese, toast and tea for

Although the sketch was done at Café de Flore in Saint-Germain-des-Prés, this flamboyant fellow could as easily have been drawn at Oliveto Café in Oakland's Rockridge district. This is my go-to café in the East Bay when I'm hungry for a taste of a chic Euro-style café in between my summer Paris visits.

the linguist—I present Ms. Taylor with my admittedly meager understanding of the symbolic link between French *pain* and the English "pain" in Christian doctrine. For this I speak in English, of course.

"Whenever one breaks bread," I begin, "the bread (*le pain*, pronounced pan with a soft nasal 'n') does not feel pain (*peine*, pronounced pen). Yet when scripture speaks of Jesus Christ as 'the bread of life' and then, on the cross, as 'broken bread'—well, that's another story."

While we wait for our food, I continue my homily. "The agony of the bread is, therefore, the agony of the cross. Fast forward through Christ's resurrection and the birth of the church to the liturgy of Holy Communion, in which the body (bread) and blood (wine) of Christ are symbolically ingested."

I am preaching to the choir and Taylor, a lapsed Catholic, stops me short. "But Jean," she asserts in her charming French-accented English, "French Catholics believe that *zee* body and blood of Christ are *literally*, not symbolically, present in *zee* bread and wine." She then translates the French saying, *nul pain sans peine* (no bread without pain). We take our bread and our pain very seriously!"

Taylor clarifies one more minor point. "The French rarely break bread with their hands. They cut bread with a knife, and usually on a diagonal."

Noted.

Our server, dressed in bohemian black, arrives with our beverages. I take notes as Taylor ventures into etymology. The French *pain* has its roots in Sanskrit and Latin. The Sanskrit *pa* (long) and *nis* (to feed or nourish) evolved into Latin as *panis*. And when we break bread with another, we are *copains*—friends. The *co* is from the Latin *cum*, meaning "with"—with bread. In English, the word "companion" literally means bread mate.

HOW YOU SAY IT MATTERS

My perfect poached eggs arrive along with Taylor's silky smoked salmon served with toast and thick Philly cream cheese. There is no Italian equivalent of American cream cheese, so Oliveto opts for the Philly, the mother of all industrial cream cheese. Taylor takes a piece of Oliveto's *levain* toast, holds it up and continues: "The word *levain* is pronounced with *zat* same nasally vowel sound as *pain*. It sounds *zee* way a French baby cries, *ouin, ouin*. English and American babies go *whaa, whaa*."

Taylor emphasizes the importance of correct pronunciation. "If you don't pronounce *zee* words correctly," she explains while spreading the cheese on a slice of toast and layering it with salmon and cucumber slices, "your server may not understand what you are ordering and express *dédain*."

French words like le *dédain* (disdain), *lapin* (rabbit), *vingt* (twenty), and of course, *pain* are all words that contain variants (ain, in, ing, etc.) of the forty different ways to write the ouin, ouin sound in French. Taylor also advises getting the French articles and genders right. "Order *la pain* instead of *le pain* and you could end up with a plate of *lapin*."

SPEAKING OF RABBITS

All this talk of pain, *pain* and *lapin* stimulates Taylor's childhood memories of the little chocolate rabbits she consumed during Easter services. Ah ha! More links. Broken bread is resurrected as chocolate lapins. Easter's rituals were associated by early Christians with the pagan celebration of spring, and rabbits are symbols of both fecundity and resurrection. The female rabbit's prodigious procreative capacities are evident, I learn, in her ability to get pregnant twice in the same season, carrying two litters simultaneously.

After my *délicieux repas* I'm feeling rather pregnant myself. I announce in my best French, *"Je suis vraiment plein"*—I am really full. (It's the ouin, ouin sound again.) Taylor, laughing, corrects me. "Plein is not used for human fullness. Rabbits can be plein, but not people. Your pockets can be full of money (*poches pleines d'argent*) but you are *repu*."

Je suis repu. I must remember this when next in Paris.

I summarize my new understanding to Ms. Taylor: "So if I eat too many chocolate rabbits, *je suis repu de lapins en chocolat*. But if I buy a box of chocolate rabbits I have *une boîte pleine de lapins en chocolat*."

"C'est ça!" Taylor agrees.

And with that my poly-lingual fashionista *professeur* rises, kisses me, a semi-poly-lingual caféista, on both cheeks and strides off. Alone again at the table, I order another latte and scan my notes. I feel the relief that always follows the intensity, and vague humiliation, of my French sessions with Lisa Taylor. My brain is full. *Mon cerveau est plein*.

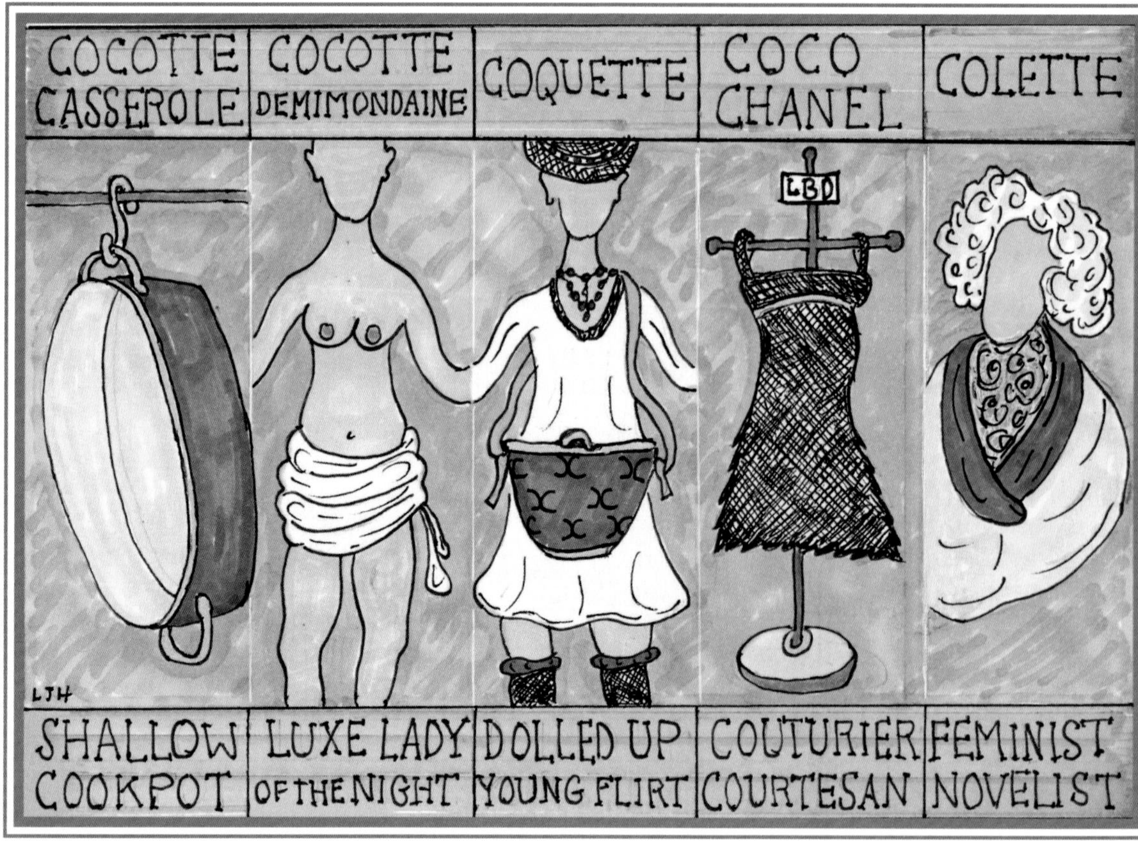
COCOTTE CASSEROLE
COCOTTE DEMIMONDAINE
COQUETTE
COCO CHANEL
COLETTE
LBD
LJH
SHALLOW COOKPOT
LUXE LADY OF THE NIGHT
DOLLED UP YOUNG FLIRT
COUTURIER COURTESAN
FEMINIST NOVELIST

La Cocotte, la Coquette and Madame Colette

Among all the modernized aspects of the most luxurious of industries, the model, a vestige of voluptuous barbarianism, is like some plunder-laden prey. She is the object of unbridled regard, a living bait, the passive realization of an ideal. No other female occupation contains such potent impulses to moral disintegration as this one, applying as it does the outward signs of riches to a poor and beautiful girl.

– Sidonie-Gabrielle Colette

From the late 17th century onward, following Francesco Procopio's invention of his café as a showcase for Parisian glamour, fashion and style, the more subversive functions of the café as a public forum for political, philosophical, amorous and artistic radicalism found caffeinated expression, even scandal and revolution, in Paris' growing inventory of cafés. The café styles of the Belle Époch (1871–1914), high and low, straddled the cultural divide between bourgeois respectability and fin-de-siècle decadence in Paris. The flip side of the *luxe* cafés of the *grande bourgeoisie* were the louche cafés of its shadowy underbelly, the *demimonde* ("half-world") of bohemian poets, decadent artists and their models, drug- and alcohol-addicted hustlers and *filles de joie* of every stripe. Whole books have been written about French decadence and the sometimes-fuzzy line between Roman Catholicism's tendencies towards both extreme piety and eroticism played out aesthetically by poets (Baudelaire), novelists (Huysmans) and artists (Moreau). In his book *Decadence and Catholicism* Ellis Hanson makes this point perfectly clear:

Catholicism is itself an elaborate paradox. . . The church is at once modern and yet medieval, ascetic and yet sumptuous, spiritual and yet sensual, chaste and yet erotic, homophobic and yet homoerotic, suspicious of aestheticism and yet an elaborate work of art.

There may be an even older influence on fin-de-siècle decadence in France than the paradoxes of the Catholic Church. Patrick Devedijian, a French deputy interviewed by Elaine Sciolino for her book *La Seduction*: "Our institutions originate in the decadence of ancient Rome."

COFFEE AS APHRODISIAC

In pre-Procope Paris, coffee was primarily an exotic Oriental beverage with powerfully stimulating properties, mostly served in private homes. Doctors of the period even prescribed coffee as an aphrodisiac. Post Procope, cafés served as caffeinated platforms for amorous liaisons. On the arms of gentlemen, the entry of elegant women from the finest Parisian salons into café society proved to be one of the most profound social advances credited to Paris' chic café culture. At the lower end of the social spectrum, the cafés of the demimonde became home to Paris' notorious filles de joie (or *filles des rues*) who plied their trade to a hungry clientele.

VOULEZ VOUS POULET AVEC MOI CE SOIR?

In French, the terminology that we lump together in English as prostitutes—hookers, whores, call girls, street walkers and tramps—is far more nuanced and hierarchical. From the lowest *pute*, *poule* (chicken), *morue* (cod) and *grue* (crane) to the top of the line *courtisane* and *grande horizontale*, the French celebrate the virtues of feminine beauty and sexuality, and they tolerate, at least until recent headline scandals (Dominique Strauss-Kahn etc.), the vices.

As portrayed in Susan Griffin's *The Book of the Courtesans* (see Lesson Six), courtesans were at the pinnacle of a hierarchy of masculine love objects treated by salon society as virtual celebrities. Near the top were *cocottes* and *grandes horizontales*. Slightly lower were the *poules de luxe* (expensive chickens) and *belles de jour* ("afternoon delights"). Lower still were the lorettes and miscellaneous *demimondaines,* including *grisettes* (working-class shop girls) who had fallen into the "half world" of modeling and/or prostitution.

I claim no scholarly or empirical expertise in these saucy semantic parsings, which are somewhat fluid from one source to the next. The important point is that the overlap between sexual and physical hunger is embedded in the French language. No surprise. A cocotte is both a fashionable prostitute and a casserole. (Susan Griffin tells the story of the celebrated courtesan Cora Pearl, who had herself served to her suitor in a giant chafing dish.) Not to be confused with the innocent *coquette*, a flirtatious girly-girl decked out seductively in fashionable accessories, both cocotte and coquette derive from *coq* (rooster)—a meal *and* a seduction.

Perhaps it goes even deeper than language. The marriage between food and sex is in France's cultural DNA. Again from *La Seduction*, Elaine Sciolino identifies the French obsession with pleasure as the common link between the two:

> *Food is consistently presented in France as a source of pleasure, and gustatory is so close to amatory*
> *delight that the lines may sometimes blur.*

DESSERT WINE | ICE CREAM MOLD | A BOMBSHELL
BEAUMES de VENISE | BOMBE GLACÉE | UNE BOMBE

In the south of France in the Rhône Valley, the town of Beaumes-de-Venise produces a celebrated sweet white wine from Muscat grapes. Beaumes is pronounced bom, not too far removed from the French word *bombe*, which is used for both atom bombs and well-endowed, usually blonde bombshells. Curiously, the French bikini swim suit got its name, according to most accounts, from the 1946 A-bomb test in the Marshall Islands on an atoll called Bikini. Blonde bombshells in bikinis had an explosive effect on male libidos.

GOURMANDISE AND GOURMANDINE

Perhaps the least known conflation in French of nutrition and procreation—life and more life—are two words, *gourmandise* and the rarely used *gourmandine*.

Gourmandise in both English and French is derived from *gourmand*, which can mean gluttony (greediness) or an appreciation of refined food (delicacies). Older than "gourmet" (early 19th century), "gourmand" (late 15th century) comes from the Old French, *groume*, or glutton.

Note that gluttony is one of Catholicism's seven deadly sins. Its meaning is nicely explicated by Saint Thomas Aquinas in his list of variations on the theme: eating too soon, too expensively, too much, too eagerly, too daintily, too wildly. I haven't seen a better description of our contemporary term in English for excessive gastronomical enthusiasm: the foodie.

Gourmandine, a corruption of *gourgandine*, is yet another quasi-gastronomic synonym for prostitute, mostly found in classical French literature. Joan DeJean explains in her book *The Essence of Style* that "gourmandine" was also the name of a new (early 17th century) bodice that revealed a woman's undergarments (*lingerie*). DeJean cleverly connects the birth of haute couture in the court of Louis XIV to the evolving function of the café as a showcase for coquettish (if not "cocottish") women and their seductive à la mode fashions.

COUTURE, COCO AND COLETTE

In this context, the word "couture" is very interesting. Meaning "stitched together" (seam), it contains the root *co*, Latin for "with." It's curious that arguably the two greatest French women of the arts to emerge in the Belle Époch period were both of the "co" variety: Gabrielle "Coco" Chanel (1883–1971) and Sidonie-Gabrielle Colette (1873–1954). Never mind that they are co-Gabrielles as well. Their celebrated lives (and romances) bridged that same cultural divide we began this lesson with: the dizzying heights of bourgeois Parisian luxe and the moral depths of Paris' demimonde.

Curious also that couturier Chanel, whose *dessins modernes* freed women from their gourmandines (bodices), earned a double "coco" (child slang for little chicken) as a nickname. Was this a reference to a lyric from the popular song she notoriously sang as a young cabaret singer, or her experience as a young quasi-cocotte (her first marriage was one of convenience, as English would have it), or her early years as an industrious seamstress and milliner?

Like Coco, our second French "co," the proto-feminist Colette spent her early years as a racy stage performer. Colette's most popular novel in English, *Gigi*, centered on the world of courtesans, former courtesans and would-be courtesans. By the end of her fabulous life, much celebrated worldwide, Colette was living in a glamorous apartment overlooking Paris' Palais-Royal where kings and queens had lived centuries earlier. Her neighbor and dear friend was the great Jean Cocteau (*Coc*-teau).

Of course, semantic analysis can't always explain the fickle and often funny trajectories of history's ironic narratives, nor why words, like memories, are created, vanish and on occasion return. Hard not to conclude, while nursing a grand crème at Café de la Mairie on place Saint-Sulpice—where, back in the day, world cinema's *Belle de Jour* (and local resident) Catherine Deneuve would often make an appearance—that the spectacle we call history is merely our vain attempt at explaining a vast unfolding of incomprehensible coincidence.

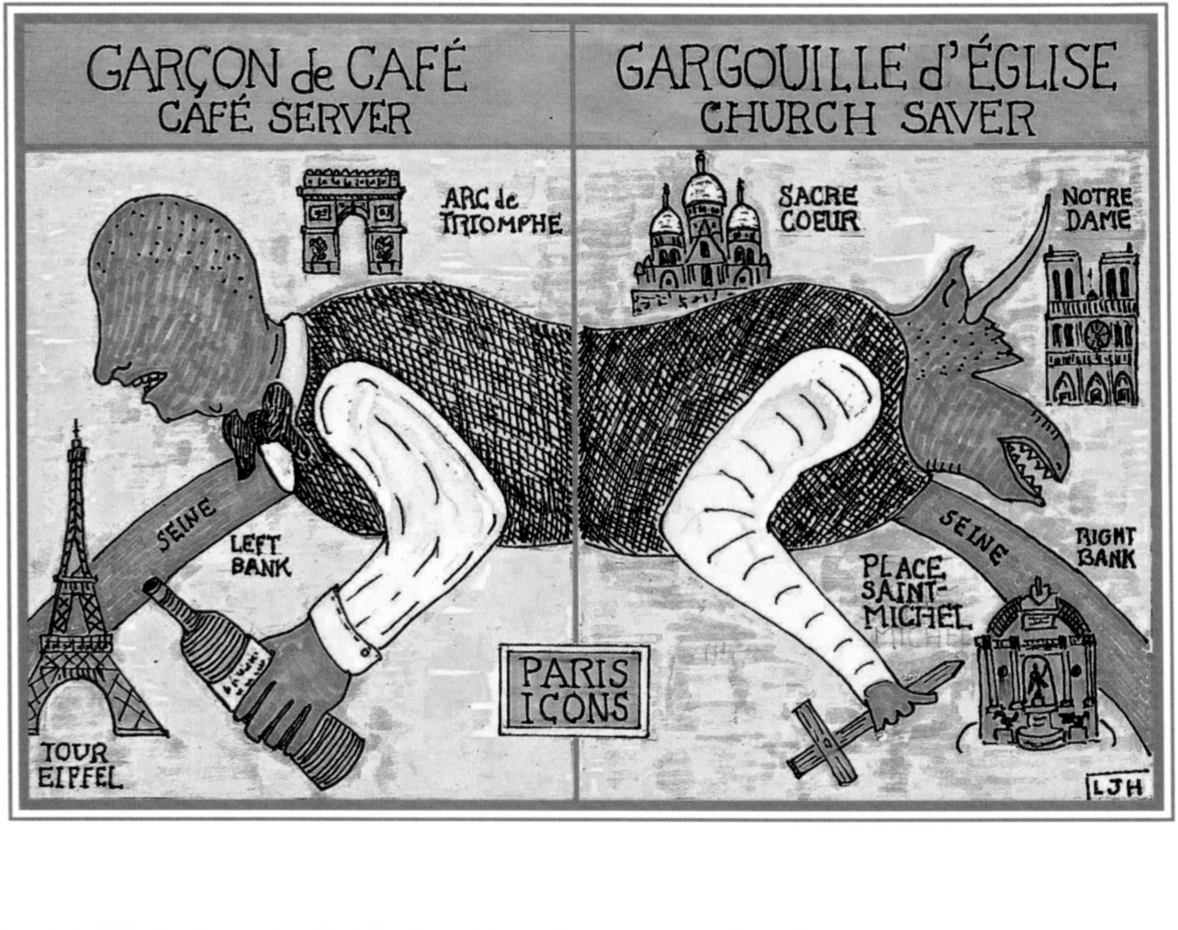
GARÇON de CAFÉ
CAFÉ SERVER
GARGOUILLE d'ÉGLISE
CHURCH SAVER
ARC de TRIOMPHE
SACRE COEUR
NOTRE DAME
SEINE
LEFT BANK
SEINE
RIGHT BANK
PLACE SAINT-MICHEL
PARIS ICONS
TOUR EIFFEL
LJH

THE GARCON, THE GARGOYLE AND GARGANTUA

To the painters, engravers, and caricaturists of that period we are particularly indebted for pictures that have added greatly to our knowledge of early coffee customs and manners.

– William Harrison Ukers
All About Coffee

Not the Eiffel Tower, the Arc of Triumph or even Notre Dame Cathedral and its gaggle of roofline gargoyles: Nothing and no one is more identified with Paris than the *garçon de café*, that black and white terror who serves forth croque monsieur, *une coupe de champagne*, café crème and a lot of attitude on almost every street in Paris. While it is a bit outdated, and using "Monsieur" may be more polite, especially for older servers, "garçon" will remain a term of art, I believe, as long as there are cafés in Paris.

At one of the most beloved corners in Paris, at boulevard Saint-Germain and rue Bonaparte in the 6th, Café Les Deux Magots offers a dramatic view of the Romanesque church Saint-Germain-des-Prés. This is my go-to café on arrival in Paris and the perfect spot from which to celebrate the often misunderstood Parisian garçon and his unique place in French culture.

Can this fellow be arrogant? Yes! Even nasty? *Très*. However, in all his varied guises throughout the centuries of French café history, the garçon is always efficient and knowledgeable, and he is never boring. Still, as reported in the *Wall Street Journal* (February 21, 2015), the city of Paris' Office of Tourism is bent on making this paragon of professionalism "nicer." To what end? To please tourists, of course.

GARÇON LITE

But if the garçon is destined for an attitudinal makeover, it will be, it seems to me, a more fraught transformation of Paris than Baron Haussmann's demolitions and reconstructions under Napoleon III. With Haussmann in charge, Paris tragically lost much of its medieval heritage and charm but gained much more in the way of hygiene (a new sewer system) and urban splendor—the grand boulevards, broad sidewalks, parks and elegant stone apartment blocks we know and love today. (Never mind the military motive for Haussmann's broader, straighter boulevards: better sight lines for army cannon, and a deterrent against barricades built by citizens during periods of political unrest and revolution. Some things never change.)

With the proposed sweetening of the garçon, the traditional Parisian café may gain tourist lucre, but at the risk of losing Gallic sizzle, in no small part due to the garçon's trademark sass.

WHEN THE DANDY MEETS THE BUTLER

The traditional café garçon is, after all, intentionally monstrous. A clever construct, he combines the self-absorbed fastidiousness of the Parisian dandy and the haughty solicitousness of the British butler. The garçon's costume is no accident. It was conceived in the early 19th century to both function and impress. His many-pocketed black vest holds money, *les additions* (café checks) and service accessories such as corkscrews, pens, crumb scoopers, etc. The still-popular bow tie adds a touch of Belle Époch panache and the air of the bon vivant. In his spotless white apron (less common today except in more upscale establishments) the garçon appears simultaneously hygienic and striking, even sexy, like a *chef de cuisine* in his crisp whites. A far cry from the pre-Procope Paris coffee servers who wore Armenian-style costumes, complete with hats trimmed in fur.

The mastery of this well-trained professional—think of those trays piled high and how orders are rarely written down—impresses and even intimidates, but at the same time seduces. He is often better dressed and more knowledgeable than his customers about French food and wine, and he knows it. The garçon exudes control, but if approached respectfully he will treat his customers well, if not cordially.

THE GARGLING GARGOYLE

Is there not, in fact, something about the café garçon that evokes that other fearsome Paris "gar," the gargoyle (*gargouille*, pronounced gar-*goo*-ya) so prominent on Gothic cathedral facades? Think about it: Both are "in service," one to the secular church (i.e., the café) and one to the sacred church. Both guard their respective terrains jealously. And like the garçon, the gargoyle is a construct, a combination of protective Gothic chimera and practical drainage technology—the first deflecting the devil, the second the rain.

Both the French and English words *gargouille* and "gargoyle" derive from the Old French *gargole*, which means gutter or waterspout and throat. Also related to goutte ("a drop") from the Latin gutta (see Lesson Seven). In the practical sense, gargoyles function at the roofline of large, usually religious structures. Water from the roof flows through gargoyle's body, exits the throat and is dumped on the ground several feet away from the structure's foundations. (Not unlike lager louts out on the town!) This protects both the church's mortared stone walls and its spiritual purity from the ill effects of "dirty" water.

RABELAIS' LITERARY GIANT, GARGANTUA

I have found no direct etymological connection between garçon and gargouille. *Garçon* first appears in the Old French *garçun* and refers to a poor boy or young servant. In the late 18th century, with the rise of the Parisian café and restaurant, the lowly garçon becomes a waiter (*serveur*).

The "gar" of gargoyle is from the Latin and means chatter, or the sounds that come from the throat or gutter. This gives us "guttural" and "gargle" and Gargantua, the young giant in Rabelais' 16th-century novel. At birth Gargantua cries out for "drink, drink, drink." His father, Lord Grangousier, noting his son's huge anatomical features (including an enormous "roger"), exclaims, "*Que grand tu as et souple le gousier*" ("How great and nimble a throat thou hast"), which becomes the name, Gar-gan-tua, and the basis of our English word "gargantuan." Rabelais adds that it takes the milk from 17,913 cows to satisfy the giant baby's thirst.

When Rabelais' narrative brings the young Gargantua to Paris, the giant is irritated by the swarms of people gathered around him as he leans up against Notre Dame. He relieves himself (a "piss-flood") and, the novel tells us, drowns 260,418 Parisians. Protective gargoyles notwithstanding, Gargantua proceeds to steal Notre Dame's bells, which he places around the neck of his giant horse before returning them.

HOMAGE TO THE GARÇON

If after 500 years we are still amused by the satirical exploits of Rabelais' trouble-making Gargantua, why can't we embrace, after centuries of French café culture, the classic, snooty garçon de café as he is? Instead of softening the garçon, let's cast him in hard, eternal bronze. Imagine as you sit at Les Deux Magots, on the terrace facing l'Église Saint-Germain, a giant statue of a garçon, a vertical gargoyle, spouting "wine" into a broad, tiled pond in the plaza between Magots and the church. The plaque at the base of the statue reads, *Vive le garçon!*

It may be wishful thinking to believe that a statue can be erected to pay homage to the garçon as a beloved and essential character in French culture. There are those today who claim the use of the term garçon is outmoded, if not offensive, preferring the supposedly less class-based terms *serveur* and *serveuse*. Nevertheless, the proposal is hereby made. *C'est possible!*

VIVE LE GARÇON!

CROQUE MONSIEUR

CROAK MONSIEUR

CROQUE MADAME

CROAK MADAME

Monsieur Croque
Loves Madame Croak

Croque-Monsieur: A rather fantastic name for a kind of hot sandwich, which is served as an hors-d'oeuvre or a small entrée. It can also feature in the list of small dishes for lunch, tea, etc.

– Larousse Gastronomique

From one arrondissement to another, as noted earlier, the Parisian café menu is fairly standardized with a mix of simple and complex dishes reflecting the hierarchy of French cusine from high to low. One finds dishes that satisfy both local demand for snacks and light meals, as well as tourist demand for larger meals and the clichés of the café menu. Two café standards, one a snack or lunch item—the *croque monsieur* and *croque madame*—and the other a lunch and dinner *plat*—roast chicken (*poulet rôti*)—are the subjects of the next two lessons. I spent two flâneurian summers in Paris tasting and reporting on these classics for my magazine.

You won't generally find such simple dishes in cookbooks devoted to Paris, a case in point being Patricia Wells' *The Paris Cookbook*. Nevertheless they are as closely identified with Paris as any of the classics, from *escargots* and pâté to *soupe à l'oignon* and *tarte tatin*. And, truth be told, though the croque monsieur and poulet rôti are not complex, they are not easy for cafés to make well, as my research revealed.

Can you judge a Parisian café by its croque? I think so. If a café can't get this simple toasted ham and cheese sandwich right, what hope is there for more ambitious fare? Having tasted dozens of croques, I am tempted to petition the city of Paris to place Monsieur and Madame Croque on an endangered species list. By and large, the croques I sampled were mediocre at best, with a few standouts, mostly at the highest price point.

The standard croque monsieur is a grilled (or toasted) ham and cheese sandwich usually made with sweet white bread called *pain de mie* and ideally dressed with either creamy *béchamel* or cheesy Mornay sauce. Grated cheese, either Swiss Gruyère or Emmenthal (but sometimes the richer Comté), is spread inside over the ham and on top of the sandwich, and then browned top and bottom (brushed with butter) until the melted cheese (with or without added sauce) starts to drip down the sides. Chic cafés often replace the pain de mie with a more rustic, artisan loaf from acclaimed bakery Poilâne.

The Italians have their paninis, the English their toasties, and the Americans their grilled cheese. But the croque monsieur is generally considered in professional food circles the king of the hill. Madame Croque is exactly the same as Monsieur, except she sports a fried-egg "hat" on her saucy head.

According to historians, this culinary couple celebrated their hundredth anniversary in 2001.

CHEESY SEMANTICS

The word *croque* comes from the French verb *croquer*, "to bite" or "to crunch." Hence the popular but awkward English translation, "crunchy mister." It's another curious semantic irony that *panini* is a word that not only identifies the Italian version of the croque, but is also the name of the 5th-century BC Hindu grammarian considered the father of linguistics Daksiputra Panini. I just love these improbable homophonic connections! Another great one, incidentally, is related to Eugène Poubelle, the 19th-century creator of modern trash collection in Paris. *Poubelle* is now the accepted French term for trash or garbage cans, with uncomfortable homophonic resonance—beautiful poo.

CROQUES ON PARADE

Here then are some of the croques I crunched at cafés in the center of Paris—the good, the bad and the inedible. I've grouped them by price because with the Parisian croque you generally get what you pay for.

CROQUES LESS THAN 8 EUROS

Le Duc d'Albret, rue Danielle-Casanova

La Fontaine, rue Cuvier

When I came across Le Duc d'Albret, a hole-in-the-wall café near avenue de l'Opéra, and saw croques on the menu starting at six euros (add one or two euros for the madame version and upscale Poilâne bread), I assumed it would be a disappointment. *Au contraire*, it was excellent, toasted (top *and* bottom with butter) by the owner in a commercial toaster oven while I watched. This croque even had béchamel in the center, giving it a creamy texture. Funky as the setup was, this was a homemade (fait-maison) croque. As the owner, Madame Madeira, explained to me, "You cannot make a croque in advance."

At La Fontaine, a friend's favorite morning mom-and-pop café near the lovely Jardins des Plantes in the 5th, their somewhat pricier croque set the stage for a string of similar disappointments—most notably croques preassembled (sometimes off premises or frozen), untoasted bottoms and with little if any bécha-mel to moisten an otherwise dry sandwich.

What good are Monsieur and Madame Croque without toasty bottoms and gooey interiors and tops? It can be done without the sauce, which a hundred years ago was not part of the recipe, but sauceless croques need lots of cheese and some butter in the toasting to produce a juicy, rich croque.

CROQUES FROM 8 TO 10 EUROS

Le Ponthieu Café, avenue Franklin Roosevelt

Café Dada, avenue des Ternes

Brasserie Les Deux Palais, boulevard du Palais

Café Les Mouettes, rue du Bac

Café La Palette, rue de Seine

This higher price point should result in a higher level of croque monsieurs. You'd expect croques at least as good as Le Duc d'Albret's, but that was not the case during my Croque Tour de Paris. At upscale Le Ponthieu, the Poilâne croque was not toasted on the bottom and there was no sign of béchamel. Too dry!

At hip Café Dada, I boldly sent back the half-toasted, sauce-free Poilâne croque and it came back a bit warmer but far from toasted. A double croquicide!

Then, at elegant Les Deux Palais, things got even worse—untoasted bottom, commercial sandwich bread, no béchamel and minimal ham. Utterly inedible!

The croque madame at Les Mouettes on charming rue du Bac was decently made, but the fried egg was overcooked. Madame Croque without her runny yolk coif? Criminal!

In the heart of the 6th arrondissement's artsy gallery scene (and near the historic École des Beaux-Arts), Café La Palette serves its open-faced croque on Poilâne's rustic sourdough bread. Mine was nicely toasted, but I don't think sourdough bread is best for croques (Poilâne's version of pain de mie is perfect). The slight sweetness of pain de mie complements the dark nutty flavor of the Gruyère cheese, which may be one of the secrets of the croque's enduring popularity.

CROQUES FROM 12 TO 16 EUROS

Café Le Select, boulevard du Montparnasse

Les Deux Magots, place Saint-Germain

La Closerie des Lilas, boulevard du Montparnasse

These three celebrated literary cafés on the Left Bank, though no longer the center of an avant-garde in Paris, all produce very good croques. The well-made and tasty Croque Select at Café Le Select is, in fact, a croque madame—there is no other choice on the menu, at least not when I was there. Vive les dames!

At Les Deux Magots, the open-faced croque had the distinction of being the only one I had this summer with a béchamel sauce redolent of nutmeg, the favored spice for this creamy white sauce. A pleasant croque.

Hemingway's haunt, La Closerie des Lilas, does not have croques on the menu, but the night I had

"I'm liable to completely repaint a canvas from square one. This approach comes from graffiti: erase, redo, erase..." Aléxone Gallerie 20 P.
Chiche portice
208 Blvd St. Germain

Hard for me to erase, start over. But from working on it. Loving the process over the result is the key. And I don't quite.

walking past on Blvd. St. Germain at 2 magots

That little roll of hair with a band to hold it together is so cute, hot actually. Is it a heart?

Her Hair

The Back of his head was like a bull dog's face without features. It's why I don't love bull dogs. They look like the back of a fat mans head with features.

I like this page, but I wish I didn't thinker those terms

July 12, 2011 7H

Seated on the terrace of Deux Magots after visiting an art exhibit up the street, I dove into my béchamel-loaded croque monsieur and considered the artist's comments on erasing his work and starting over. And again, more back-of-the-head sketches in my journal including a provocative "bun" on a young women walking past the café.

133

dinner there they were serving gratis at the bar (as *hors-d'œuvres*) tiny toothpicked croque monsieur squares, buttery and properly toasted. Delicious. The night after my meal at the Closerie, I served my dinner guests hors-d'œuvre-sized croque squares expertly made by a visiting friend from Berkeley, the chef Peter Jackson, who used imported Italian truffled ham, a fine aged Gruyère and a perfectly-executed béchamel sauce. Croquelicious!

CROQUES OVER 20 EUROS

Café de la Paix, place de l'Opéra

Café Fouquet's, avenue des Champs-Élysées

For twenty euros and above, a croque should be everything a croque can be—and much more. This was indeed the case at Café de la Paix, a fashionable café/restaurant with Belle Époch interiors and a literary history dating back to the 1860s. The Paix croque tasted like rich pastry. The moist interior, adequate béchamel and well-toasted top and bottom provided an explosion of flavor and texture. The pain de mie was sliced thinner than with most croques I sampled, to the sandwich's crispy advantage, and the ham a bit thicker, which gave added flavor and texture. The presentation was impressive. The center was cut out of the croque body and served as a separate "croquette." Green salad was stuffed into the body's circular void. Excellent *pommes frites* came in a separate basket.

This became my benchmark for a great Parisian café croque. Although ridiculously expensive, the Paix croque was eight euros less and much more satisfying than the double-decker monster croque at elite watering hole Café Fouquet's, on the Champs-Élysées. Sure, the Fouquet's croque was enough for four eaters and came with salad, excellent frites and several mini *financier* dessert cakes at the end. But the sandwich itself, again on the dry side, does not sit as high in my pantheon of Parisian croques as Café de la Paix's tour de force.

WILL THE PARISIAN CROQUE CROAK?

Something has to be done to save the Parisian croque, especially in the range of 8 to 10 euros. If a good croque cannot be made profitably at that price, it should not be on the café's menu.

I mention in Lesson Eleven the official Parisian tourism office's efforts to boost the sagging fortunes of traditional Parisian cafés by transforming the often arrogant and unfriendly garçon de café into a nicer tourist-friendly fellow. I suggest, instead, that the grand panjandrums of Parisian tourism apply their resources to improving Monsieur Croque, not Monsieur Garçon, who is just fine the way he is. Why not create AOC guidelines (*Appelation d'Origine Contrôlée*) for the croque monsieur, as for wine, cheese, eggs and other important French products?

CROQUE MONSIEUR LABELING REQUIREMENTS

For a sandwich to be labeled on a Parisian menu as a croque monsieur or croque madame, it must be, irrespective of price:

- Assembled on premises
- Cooked to order
- Made with Swiss Gruyère, Emmental or Comté
- Buttered in the toasting or grilling process
- Browned on both the top and bottom
- Made with either béchamel or Mornay sauce
- Made with artisanal French ham
- Made with fresh eggs for the croque madame

Enforcing the clear guidelines would help elevate the moribund Parisian croque monsieur above its current inconsistent level and begin the process of restoring the Parisian café to its former gastronomic glory one croque at a time.

Be careful to emphasize the second syllable's "ay" sound in poulet. If you say "pool-ee" you may get a stern or just confused look from your server thinking you're a worker come to hoist something to an upper floor. *Poulie* is the French word for "pulley."

TO POULET OR NOT TO POULET IN PARIS

What a deceptively simple dish. I had come to believe that one can judge the quality of a cook by his or her roast chicken. Above all, it should taste like chicken: it should be so good that even a perfectly simple, buttery roast should be a delight.

– Julia Child

Though not the most exciting selection on the standard Parisian café menu, roast chicken (*poulet rôti*, pronounced pool-*ay* ro-*ti*) is one of the best ways, as with the croque monsieur, to judge a café's culinary competence. Unlike the croque monsieur, however, whose sins can be covered up beneath its cheesy sauce, a roast chicken cannot hide.

If I apply the roast chicken test, I'm afraid I'll have to assign an overall grade of "C–" to the Parisian versions I tasted in cafés and restaurants visited in my survey. The few standout "A+" *poulets rôtis* offset the numerous "Fs", which were more abundant in cafés than restaurants. In fact, roast chicken is the last dish I would advise anyone to gamble their euros (or their health) on in Parisian cafés. You will likely have better luck at full-scale restaurants, especially those that brag about their birds' pedigreed origins, though this is no guarantee either.

The problem is not the quality of the birds. *Au contraire*, the quality is generally very high in Paris. It's the execution—often overcooked (no doubt precooked), rubbery-skinned, rather dry hunks of meat. I proactively canceled an order of roast chicken at the popular café Le Pré aux Clercs, yet another Hemingway haunt in the 6th, after seeing an unappetizing half-bird served to a table next to mine. I don't eat gray, flaccid chicken.

It's sad because the French do take their chicken—like their *liberté*—very, very seriously. In fact, they appear to equate the two. The national symbol of France, dating to the French revolution, is the rooster—*le coq gaulois*. After centuries of painstaking breeding, and prized for its depth of flavor, the most acclaimed chicken in France remains the white-feathered *poulet de Bresse*, which sports a red coxcomb and has blue legs and feet. Patriotism in France is bottom-up.

DOES A CHICKEN HAVE LIPS?

No surprise, then, that the signature French cigarette brand, Gauloise, features a highly stylized chicken logo on its blue package. The national motto of France—*liberté, égalité, fraternité*—was printed on that blue package back in the day when a New Wave movie star, Jean-Paul Belmondo, was often seen onscreen with a Gauloise dangling from his full, pouty lips. Were these his natural lips or were they the puffed-up effects, so to speak, of a Gauloise addiction? Hard to say, and in the age of botox the pouty lips one sees on fashionable women smokers in Paris are *de rigueur*. Luckily for us practicing café flâneurs the cigarette and cigar smoking has been moved outside to the sidewalk tables.

STICKER SHOCK

As staple food and cherished symbol of freedom, the humble, often comedic chicken is at the very foundation of French culture and identity. King Henri IV knew this well when, in the 16th century, he called for a chicken in every peasant's pot. Today, this can be translated as a roast chicken on every café menu and at every *traiteur*, *boucherie* and *marché*.

Poultry symbolism aside, getting a handle on France's highly evolved farm-raised poultry industry (*poulet fermier*) and its exhaustively- and sometimes confusingly-labeled products seems to require an advanced degree in agricultural science, if not French culture and linguistics.

Among the most pampered chickens in France, perched at the pinnacle of France's poultry hierarchy, are birds *élevés en libertés* or "born to be free." This term is proudly printed on the colorful labels attached to pricey packages of poultry sold under France's Label Rouge certification program. (The program is controversial in some circles, but then in France everything is controversial for some group or other, except France itself!)

It's no accident that the term adopted for the country's premium birds (*liberté*) appears first, ahead of both *égalité* and *fraternité*, in France's national motto. It took almost the entire 19th century for the sequence of the French Revolution's tripartite motto to become fixed. Use of the term liberté to identify and market France's finest poultry was set in motion in the 1960s, when the Label Rouge program was launched.

FRENCH CHICKENS A LITTLE LESS FREE

The liberté-raised birds are allowed to roam outdoors without fences or time restrictions. "Totally free" is another translation for *élevé en liberté*. Accordingly, these birds command the highest prices in French shops, save for organic (*bio*) poultry and specialty birds like those from the region around Bourg-en-Bresse in the east of France, which are AOC-protected and produced under conditions even more demanding than those for Label Rouge.

Moreover, there is no one-term-fits-all label in France for free-range birds as in the U.S. where progressive poultry production is, according to one industry spokesperson I talked to, twenty-five years behind France. An existential notch below chickens *élevés en libertés* are those *élevés en plein air*, or raised out-of-doors. These plein air chickens (and ducks, geese, turkeys, etc.) are required under the Label Rouge program to have ample time to range outside their coops within a fenced but generous area of no less than twenty-one square feet per bird. The U.S. Department of Agriculture's more lax standards require only that free-range poultry producers give their birds unspecified and unverified time outdoors with no space requirements. Home, home on the range? Well, at least once in awhile, if they are lucky.

Note that plein air is the same term used to describe the Impressionist landscape painting style that liberated oil painting from the confines and subject matter of academic studio painting. The cafés of 19th-century Montmartre were filled with free-range painters!

FROM A FRENCH EXISTENTIALIST PERSPECTIVE

The freedom- and chicken-loving French may be all about liberty for themselves and their winged comestibles, but no matter how strict and humane the regulations under a certification program like Label Rouge, the chickens in France are far from free, existentially speaking. Chickens and all their related galliformes, whether free-range or factory-farmed, are bred, raised, slaughtered, labeled and consumed at the complete whim—and profit—of humans. As one Parisian butcher put it to me when I asked a lot of questions about the chicken I was investing in—a lovely plein air bird raised just outside the Bresse appellation, and thus at a more palatable price—"If chickens were really free to range they would take off and never return." I laughed and shot back a gallinaceous variation on Jean-Paul Sartre's iconic line from his existentialist play *No Exit*, "Yeah, hell is other chickens."

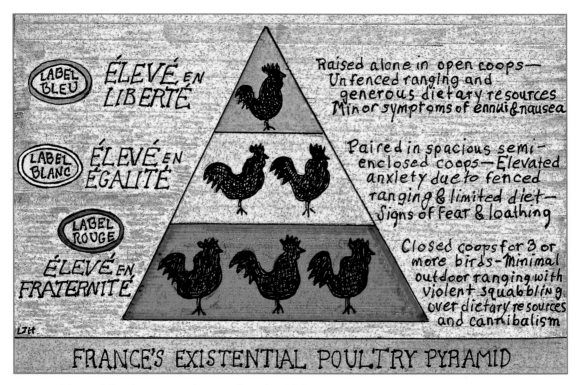

FRANCE'S EXISTENTIAL POULTRY PYRAMID

Any resemblance of this chart to any other French poultry labeling system is purely coincidental.

SOME FOWL EXPERIENCES IN PARIS

All existential considerations aside—along with the euphemistic terminology used by compassionate (and clever) carnivores to market chicken—in order to fully appreciate the gastronomic virtues of the bird, one still has to cook it, and cook it well.

If Paris celebrates its roast chicken, I have found that the restaurants doing most of the bragging are often the most wanting. Here are two empty boasters and one exceptional purveyor I visited on my recent free-range tour of Paris poulet.

A TALE OF TWO BIRDIES

At celebrity chef Guy Savoy's L'Atelier Maître Albert in the 5th, the handsome, wall-sized rôtisserie had two enticing birds (from the Landes region) seductively turning on their spit, just waiting for me, right? Wrong. About twenty-five minutes after ordering the *Volaille fermière rôtie*, my two small so-so-tasting chicken pieces, a small leg and quarter breast, arrived nestled against a typical mound of buttery bistro *pommes purée*. Those lovely lovebirds, still spinning side-by-side as I left, were apparently all show and no go. A poulet tease! So where had *my* chicken pieces come from? The stork? A surreptitious closer look (Investigative Journalism 101) revealed that the chicken being served that night came from a stainless steel warming drawer below the rôtisserie. How long had these chickens been waiting for me? The secret to good roast chicken is that it must be cooked and served to order, and cafés and restaurants, with few exceptions, don't—perhaps can't for a number of practical and economic reasons—do that.

SHADOWS OF JAMES BEARD'S BIRD

Equally disappointing was the Provençal-style roast chicken with thyme and whole cloves of garlic touted at La Bastide Odéon in the 6th. The traditional Provençal combination of chicken and garlic was popularized in the U.S. by folks like James Beard with their variations on the classic poulet *aux quarante gousses d'ail* (chicken with forty cloves of garlic). Either Beard was dreaming, or there was a recent garlic blight in

France, because my skinless chunks of white meat and a small leg were served with just *one* clove of garlic! It hadn't even caramelized into that soft, sweetly nutty puddle of garlic heaven one expects with this much-loved preparation. And what was with the *skinless* breast meat? Poulet rôti sacrilège! For me, I confess, the whole point of properly roasted chicken is the crisp skin.

CHICKEN FLYING HIGH

Of the many poulets rôtis I gobbled at cafés and restaurants during my tour, the only real standout was the whole chicken for two at Chez l'Ami Louis in the 3rd (85 euros!). This is the notoriously high-end, old-school bistro that food critics love to hate. A. A. Gill labeled it "the worst restaurant in the world" in his giddy 2010 *Vanity Fair*-thrashing of the place, which was inducement enough for me to go. I'm a bit of an ambulance chaser when it comes to hatchet job reviews of reputable restaurants—I like to see (and taste) the damage for myself. On occasion, such as this one, I like to write rebuttals.

Not only was L'Ami Louis' bird (a black-legged Label Rouge "noir" bird from the Challans region) moist and flavorful, and its delicate skin crisp, but the bird was graciously served (Gill found the servers at L'Ami Louis "sullen") in two brilliant courses that followed a ceremonial presentation of the whole uncarved bird at the table—white meat first, then dark—both accompanied by ladles of perfect *jus*. If anything at L'Ami Louis was sullen, it was the limp mound of pommes frites served with the chicken. But who cares! The bird is the word.

My guest at l'Ami Louis, the expat editor David Jester, had resisted the idea of my spending so much money on a dish one could make just as well at home for a fraction of the cost. In fact, he boasted, at *his* home. My argument was that I couldn't write about chicken in Paris without going to l'Ami Louis, and I couldn't go alone. Chicken for two, don't you know? But to his surprise, David loved the place, the service and most importantly, the chicken. Not so much, however, that he didn't repeat his boast that his wife, Evy, could match or beat it. I accepted his invitation.

ALL YOU NEED IS LOVE, LOVE, LOVE

Fast forward to David and Evy's cozy apartment near Place Monge in the 5th and one of the tastiest, and surely the most love-infused, roast chickens I had during my chicken-lickin' tour of Paris. Our Label Rouge plein air bird labeled *jaune* (yellow)—a young female with yellow skin and feet, purchased from a boucherie near their apartment—was raised in the Ain region in eastern France, where celebrity Bresse chickens come from. After ninety minutes in the oven, the coarse-salt-rubbed five-pound bird had deliciously golden, crisp skin and juicy, rosemary-scented meat. Evy, a passionate and talented advocate of *cuisine du marché*, served the bird with the pan juices and the caramelized carrots, garlic cloves (lots!) and lemon rind that had roasted alongside the bird for the last hour in the oven. Poulet perfection.

Evy says that the secret of her chicken's succulent flesh and crisp skin, learned from her butcher, is to start the bird out in a *cold* oven set at 400 degrees, a technique designed to keep the white meat moist. A successful method, to be sure. But Evy's real secret, I believe, which I think too many Parisian restaurant chefs and café operators have sadly forgotten, is that to do justice to pedigreed poultry you must—and I say this at the risk of sounding pathetically Berkeley—*love* poulet rôti, *love* taking the time to make it well and *love* those you are serving.

I have modified this iconic image of Balzac (left), a daguerreotype by Nadar from 1842, to show Balzac holding a demitasse, his reported coffee cup of choice. By today's measure, his addiction of 40–50 cups per day represents about 10–12 6 oz. cups, a heavy caffeine burden on his system that may have contributed to his death. The original Nadar photo shows Balzac's open left hand resting on his chest, a characteristic pose at the time. The coffee pot with Balzac's initials (right) is on display at the Maison de Balzac museum in the 16th, housed where the great man lived out the last years of his life.

Caffeinated Balzac, Beau Brummell and the Blue Death

Coffee is very much in use in Paris: there are public houses where it is distributed. In some of these houses one talks of news, in others one plays chess. There's one where coffee is prepared in such a way that it gives spirit to those who drink it.

– Charles de Montesquieu

Whoever does not visit Paris regularly will never really be elegant.

– Honoré de Balzac

In this lesson I am examining the coffee/café dialectic, switching from semantic investigations to a more historical perspective. Spotlighted are several 18th- and 19th-century characters to help me deconstruct the relationship between coffee, the beverage and the café as a *theatrum mundi* ("All the world's a stage"): chiefly, three cultural superheroes—Honoré de Balzac, Jean Anthelme Brillat-Savarin and Beau Brummell—with brief appearances by the revolutionary Camille Desmoulins, the historian George Sainsbury and lastly the medical researcher Thomas Latta, a somewhat minor character who nevertheless deserves to be better known.

While it's true that the word "café" in French signifies both the place and the product, underscoring the historical connection between coffee consumption and café culture, it's not at all true that café-goers drink only coffee or that drinking coffee requires a café. Both sides of the word, so to speak, are broader than that. Coffee-phobic café-goers have consumed all kinds of stimulating beverages in cafés for hundreds of years, from wine and absinthe to chocolat chaud and soft drinks. And there are those coffeeholics whose attachment to coffee is strictly a domestic affaire.

Bridging the thin line between irony and the absurd, the world-historical character most identified with prodigious, perhaps pathological coffee consumption appears not to have been a café regular at all—except, perhaps, for sumptuous meals at legendary Paris cafés like Tortoni's, Café Riche and Café de Paris. He may not even have been a fan of the beverage's taste. I speak of course of Honoré de Balzac, whose over-caffeinated genius gave us *La Comédie humaine*'s portraits of French society that still seem unimaginable in their voluminous brilliance. How could anyone produce almost a hundred mostly great novels (according to critics who have managed to read them all) in a lifespan of just fifty-one years and a prime productive period of just twenty? I will answer my own question: coffee. Gallons of coffee. Dark rivers of coffee. A universe of coffee consumed mostly at home.

According to legend, Balzac would fuel his eighteen-hour writing binges by downing up to fifty cups of filter-dripped coffee. He drank his coffee from demitasse cups, it must be noted, equivalent to about ten or twelve of our modern cups per day. Any gastronomic pleasure derived from coffee as a beverage would seem to have been of secondary importance to Balzac, if important at all. In his hilariously bombastic essay about his addiction, titled "The Pleasures and Pains of Coffee," the extraction is portrayed as a powerful, magical elixir, not a pleasant and bracing beverage:

> *As Brillat-Savarin has correctly observed, coffee sets the blood in motion and stimulates the muscles;*
>
> *it accelerates the digestive processes, chases away sleep, and gives us the capacity to engage a little*
>
> *longer in the exercise of our intellects.*

True enough, though the magic is better understood today from a physiological point of view—that is, caffeine's ability to release pleasurable endorphins and stimulating adrenalin. After multiple readings of the essay, what is notable to me is that not once does Balzac mention anything to do with the *taste* of coffee or any pleasure in it. *Pas une seule fois* (not once). Which is all the more curious given that Balzac references the 19th-century author of *The Physiology of Taste*, his older contemporary, Jean Anthelme Brillat-Savarin, the witty gastronomer who more or less invented modern culinary sensibility with the immortal words:

"Tell me what you eat and I will tell you what you are." In Balzac's case, Brillat-Savarin would have to conclude, "a caffeine-addicted, coffee-eating glutton." Yes, Balzac *ate* ground coffee in order to magnify its stimulating effect in the face of the caffeine tolerance that developed.

When Balzac ventured out into the world to purchase his coffee, he was selective. According to the author of *Balzac: A Biography*, Graham Robb notes:

> *Balzac's special blend of coffee required a visit to several Parisian grocers and half a day's shopping.*
>
> *The local variety was insipid: "No great inspirations to be had with this coffee," he complained.*

Again, nothing is said about taste, only effect (inspiration). If Balzac appreciated Brillat-Savarin's elevated Epicureanism, he didn't seem to share in it.

In another confirmation of Balzac's narrow, non-gastronomic perspective on coffee, and on food in general, Anka Muhlstein writes in her book *Balzac's Omelette: A Delicious Tour of French Food and Culture with*

Honoré de Balzac that the author's focus on food was more about social observation than taste:

> *If you want to imagine savoring an oyster as it melts on your tongue, read Maupassant; if you dream of jugs filled with yellow cream, try Flaubert; and if the thought of beef in aspic tickles you, turn to Proust. But if you are interested not so much in the taste of the oyster as in the way a young man orders it, less the cool sweetness of the cream than how much it costs, and less the melting quality of the aspic than what it reveals about how the household is run, then read Balzac.*

One is therefore not surprised by reports of Balzac's gluttony, suggesting, perhaps, a food addiction on top of the well-documented caffeine addiction. Binge coffee consumption fueling binge-writing episodes followed by binge eating.

PORTRAIT OF THE ARTIST AS A HOMEBODY

Balzac lived in a Paris where café culture had achieved much of the legendary status we celebrate today. The Enlightenment delivered the Parisian café as a haven for philosophers and writers like Voltaire and Diderot who, we have seen, made their home in Paris' oldest café, Le Procope, in the Latin Quarter. The French Revolution was plotted in establishments like the Palais Royal's Café Foy where Camille Desmoulins, a journalist and radical pamphleteer—and who would later be guillotined during the Terror—gave a fiery speech standing on a table in front of the café that ignited the storming of the Bastille. The post revolutionary period saw cafés inundated with bohemian artists and writers, beginning with the Romantics and Realists, followed by the Impressionists and then the Symbolists, Fauves, Dadaists and Surrealists. It was inevitable that bourgeois groupies would flow into their cafés, following like pilot fish in the wake of these larger-than-life characters.

The decades leading up to the Belle Époch (1871–1914) were those in which Paris was solidifying its position as the culinary and artistic capital of Europe. The twenty years of Balzac's most prolific production—from about 1830 to 1850, just before his death from complications of caffeine poisoning, according to Balzac's doctor—witnessed the beginnings of an artistic avant-garde aligned with what would later evolve into modernisme and Modern Art. Much of the new art (theory, practice and product) would be developed and promoted in the cafés of Montparnasse, Montmartre, the Latin Quarter and Saint-Germain-des-Prés.

Flâneurs too evolved during this period. From strolling loafers and wealthy boulevardiers during the first part of the 19th century, flâneurs emerged along with mass circulation newspapers as working journalists. Balzac was no doubt the greatest of these. However, living and working in the Marais on the Right Bank until late in life, Balzac was more the homebody (*casanier*) than a daily café habitué. Although connected socially and professionally to many of the great artists and writers of his time (Rodin, Hugo, Baudelaire, Delacroix, Gautier), he inhabited a domestic world somewhat cut off from the society he meticulously chronicled. George Sainsbury, an early Balzac authority, wrote in an introduction to an English translation (1901) of *The Human Comedy*:

[Balzac] does not figure frequently or eminently in any of the genuine gossip of the time as a haunter of literary circles, and it is very nearly certain that the assiduity with which some of his heroes attend salons and clubs had no counterpart in his own life. In the first place he was too busy; in the second he would not have been at home there. . . He felt it his business not to frequent society but to create it.

Part of the story is that Balzac had money problems, as pointed out in Henry C. Shelly's 1912 book, *Old Paris: It's Social, Historical and Literary Associations.* Commenting on Balzac's visits to Café de Paris on boulevard des Italiens to eat the grand café's "recuperative" *veau à la casserole* after a "spell of hard work," Shelly concludes, "The visits of Balzac, however, were spasmodic, as might be inferred from the constantly chatotic condition of his finances."

Balzac may have had little time or funds for Paris' thriving café and salon society but he was sufficiently exposed to it to write in exquisite detail—much of it from his imagination, according to Sainsbury—about the social types that inhabited these worlds. This was the birth of literary realism in the 19th century with Balzac as its founding genius.

TWO TYPES: ARTIST AND DANDY

This was also the age of *les physiologies*, the cheap, pocket-sized illustrated texts that exposed and caricatured various social types: the artist, the dandy, the lawyer, the teacher, the banker, the flâneur, the courtesan, the grisette, etc. More expensive, leather-bound anthologies of this material were sold to the wealthy. These were prototypes of our deluxe coffee table books, on display in *haut bourgeois* Parisian households. Balzac the journalist, a contributor to these popular works and himself the artist type, greatly admired Charles Baudelaire, the flâneur type, and Beau Brummell, the model for the dandy type.

Balzac's ambivalent aspirations to the refined elegance of Beau Brummell is expressed in his clever but unfinished *Treatise on Elegant Living*, inspired by the notorious British fashionista. Putting himself into the context (if not the clothing) of Brummell's dandy, Balzac writes, "The artist is an exception . . . he is elegant and slovenly in turn; he dons, as he pleases, the plowman's overalls, and determines the tails worn by the man in fashion; he is not subject of laws: he imposes them."

"Exceptional" Balzac was, with an emphasis on the slovenly end of the spectrum despite his flirtation with the dandy: Brummell's carefully constructed sartorial protest against Regency aristocrats and the British upper-class fops who looked down on him for his low birth. Brummell's fashion genius and scornful wit attracted King George IV, for whom he was a fashion advisor, and launched later versions of the type like Oscar Wilde.

The following physical description of Balzac via one Captain Reese Howell Gronow, a follower of Brummell, writing his memoir of life in Paris, betrays Balzac's true nature:

The great enchanter was one of the oiliest and commonest looking mortals I ever beheld; being short and corpulent, with a broad florid face, a cascade of double chins, and straight greasy hair. . . [He] dressed in the worst possible taste, wore sparkling jewels on a dirty shirt front, and diamond rings on unwashed fingers.

Notwithstanding his appearance, Balzac's prose was just dandy. And that's what counts.

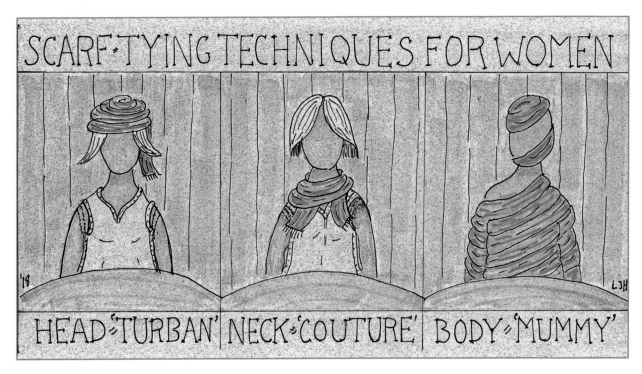

SCARF·TYING TECHNIQUES FOR WOMEN

HEAD-'TURBAN' NECK-'COUTURE' BODY-'MUMMY'

Scarves are always the rage in Paris both for men and women. Beyond sartorial display, their historical function has been to keep Frenchmen warm both in their drafty apartments and outdoors. One of the things I've had to learn to look and feel French in Paris is

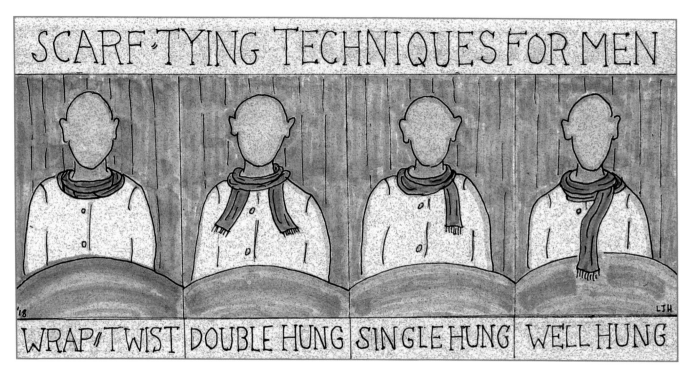

SCARF·TYING TECHNIQUES FOR MEN

| WRAP/TWIST | DOUBLE HUNG | SINGLE HUNG | WELL HUNG |

how to tie my scarf. There are countless wrapped and knotted variations, especially for women. I've sketched just a few of my favorite and easiest arrangements, including one I use to get chuckles when asked about it.

DRIP DRIP DRIP COFFEE

It's curious that at the beginning of Balzac's great literary output of the 1830s, fueled by coffee made using a variety of drip brewing devices of the period, there was another drip technology being developed in medical circles—intravenous saline drip. It was the invention of the Scotsman Thomas Latta to treat victims of the cholera pandemic, the Blue Death, raging in Europe at the time. Cholera was labeled such because the illness turned the victim's dehydrated body blue. By 1832, 20,000 Parisians and a total of 100,000 Frenchmen had been consumed by the highly contagious cholera bacterium. But just as Balzac was gearing up his assault on literary history, the pandemic eased in Europe and Latta's discoveries were forgotten until the 20th century.

Thanks to the vagaries of technological progress, Balzac never had a chance to engage with this early drip technology, assuming it could have been applied to his caffeine habit. Of course I jest, but just imagine how much more prolific Balzac might have been without spending all that time shopping for his favorite beans, grinding them, brewing them and then cleaning those fifty-odd demitasses every day. This was a lot of work for someone who didn't seem to notice the pleasure of coffee as a beverage. Why not cut to the chase and hook up to a drip line during working hours? With the saving of so much time and effort, Balzac might have finished all the work left at his premature death in 1850 and brought *The Human Comedy* to its fullest completion—the 137 books he had originally planned.

BRANDING BALZAC

A century and a half after his death, Balzac's name has become so identified with coffee that a German roaster and its chain of *kaffeebars* has burst onto the scene, the Balzac Coffee Company. Think about it: Balzac's literary brand co-opted by a coffee brand. How postmodern can you get? Is it totally lost on German coffee consumers that Balzac was a self-destructive caffeine addict, not a coffee connoisseur? Who cares, the branding works! Except perhaps for the would-be logo on the inevitable merchandise that might follow—baseball caps, coffee mugs and T-shirts. Imagine an *honest* Balzac Coffee Company T-shirt that is true to Balzac's home-boy, non-gastronomic coffee addiction. It would have to say "Stay caffeinated!" on the front and on the back, "Stay home!"

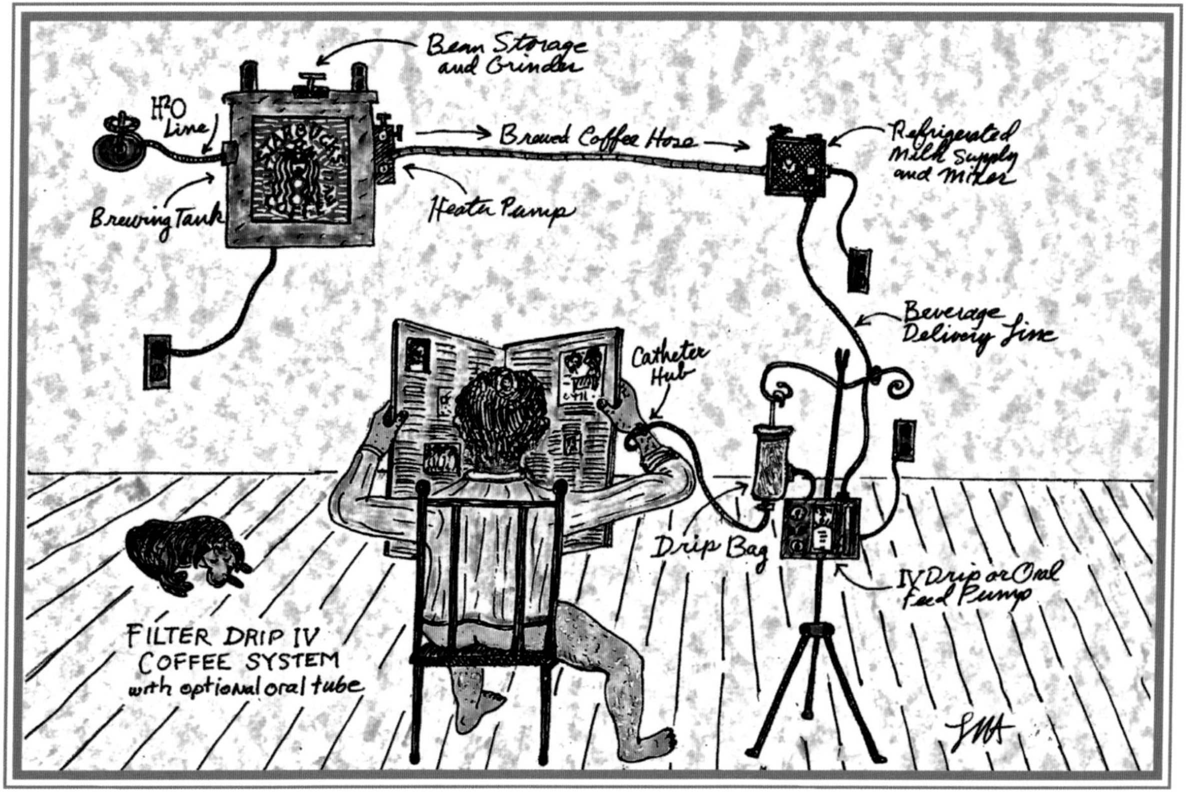
Bean Storage and Grinder
H2O Line
Brewed Coffee Hose
Refrigerated Milk Supply and Mixer
Brewing Tank
Heater Pump
Beverage Delivery Line
Catheter Hub
Drip Bag
IV Drip or Oral Feed Pump
FILTER DRIP IV COFFEE SYSTEM with optional oral tube
LMA

The Flâneur Comes Home

For my part, I am going to the cafe. A cafe is neutral territory . . . the detached and elevated sphere of the literary man, in which one is capable only of refined ideas.

– Thomas Mann

Instead of slouching in a café ignorant of the word for ice, I will head down to the coffee shop and the waitress known as Dot.

– Billy Collins
Consolation

Living the magical café culture lifestyle in Paris leads inevitably to the flâneur's fate—coming home. And coming home for this flâneur means coming down, at least for a month or two during the reentry period. Although Francophiles long for the euphoria of a Proustian "time regained" world, we live most of our quotidian lives in real time. My returns home from Paris usher in a darkish mood that colors my real-time life in Berkeley, which ten or eleven months of the year is heaven on earth.

It's always surprising to me while in my peevish post-Paris funks how hard I struggle to maintain a connection to an authentic Parisian café culture lifestyle. Berkeley, the spiritual home of the American foodie and a deep love for all things French, seems more interested in the coffee than the culture. But then this is not a European capital. Berkeley is a small college town, and a young one at that (it turned 150 in 2018). There is no "crowd" here for a flâneur to disappear into, and nothing like Haussmann's cityscape to stroll and observe—no grand boulevards or elegant public gardens and a rather modest inventory of dramatic *Beaux-Arts* buildings, mostly on the University of California campus.

The flâneur as we think of him today doesn't translate easily, if at all, into a contemporary American context. The most critical comment I've ever read about the Parisian flâneur as a thread in the urban fabric of his city is voiced by the American sociologist Jamin Creed Rowan in his influential book *The Sociable City*:

> *The flâneur views other urbanites as commodities to be consumed rather than as individuals to whom he has emotional or ethical obligations.*

This strikes me as true but ironic given that one of the historic flâneur's chief missions was to observe and resist the increasing commodification of a growing consumer society. He is then, given Rowan's view, both witness and perpetrator. But how could a flâneur in 19th-century Paris even imagine the idea of "fellow-feelings" that Rowan supports in his work on American city dwellers?

Although college town Berkeley is not an urban "city of light," it does have natural beauty in spades. Berkeley is literally carved out of nature, a very special nature comprising bay waters and streams, oak-

and boulder-studded hillsides, and forest redwoods. There are lovely little parks and elegant Arts & Crafts domestic structures encircling the UC Campus—as well as some extraordinary hundred-year-old churches—all designed by architectural heavyweights like Maybeck, Morgan, Thomas, Howard and Ratcliff. The sunsets to the west, towards the Golden Gate, and the views of Baghdad by the Bay from the Berkeley and Oakland hills are breathtaking tribute to the spiritual legacy of the Native Americans who dwelled here centuries ago.

But back home from Paris I miss the artsy gravitas and sexy sophistication of Paris' built and cultural environments. Sure, urban San Francisco is a mere bridge away from Berkeley. But the city strikes me as cut off, another universe entirely and, although exciting in its own right, nothing like Paris. San Francisco was labeled "The Paris of the West" in the 19th century (ambitious, even wishful thinking, I'd say) and today is the official Sister City to Paris, re-asserted recently by both cities' mayors. Yes, San Francisco, vying with Boston, is the most "European" of our cities, but few European cities can claim to be Paris-like either. For flâneurs and would-be expats like me, there is just nothing quite like gay Paris and its centuries-old café culture.

En route to my morning café in North Berkeley's barely fifty-year-old "gourmet ghetto," I stroll past a shop called Beauty & Gratitude, currently Berkeley's only lingerie shop. Its window display screams (or merely moans) "Soviet bloc circa 1950." It's as if this really very nice shop is afraid to be what it is. A clerk tells me it's a "lingerie boutique." But how can lingerie be so disassociated from sex? The window display hides the lingerie bits and pieces in a sea of sleepwear, promoting *la sublimation*, not France's trademark la séduction. The name says it all: "beauty" is eroticism euphemized, and "gratitude" blends Berkeley's bifurcated ethos of Christianity and Buddhism.

After a summer in haute couture Paris, Berkeley's "de-nuded" window displays seem drab, to say the least. How can one be a flâneur without exciting things to look at, whether architectural, erotic or culinary? Our food can be exciting on the plate and the palate, for sure, but nothing is really on display here, at least not like in Paris. Paris is a virtual urban topography of color, texture and form. Perhaps the core difference between the two cities is that between Roman Catholic Paris with its decadent underbelly, and historically Protestant Berkeley with its progressive political correctness. Oversimplification? All I know is that in Paris I can walk the walk of the flâneur with ease because I am literally strolling in his historical and metaphorical footsteps, looking at the things he looked at over two centuries ago—beautiful buildings, beautiful store fronts, beautiful food, beautiful women. No wonder that back in Berkeley the only flâneurs I see are in magazine ads, not on the streets.

Embedded in my ennui, I feel closer to Balzac, the caffeine-addicted homebody, than Baudelaire, the opium-addicted poet of the streets. Of course my identification with Balzac in foodista Berkeley has more to do with Balzac's gluttonous input than his unmatched literary output. In a town identified with an American coffee revolution (Peet's Coffee), Balzac is a branded bridge between our young, caffeinated digital creatives and the mythic dimension of coffee's historical narrative (café bohemians, dandies, flâneurs, etc.). In an article I wrote soon after returning from Paris a few summers ago, I chronicled an experience at Peet's that put the Paris/Berkeley café/coffee divide into stark focus. This was at Peet's on Vine Street, the original, which along with the Cheese Board Collective and Chez Panisse launched the gourmet ghetto in the 1970s and the California cuisine revolution, proclaimed in the 1980s, somewhat grandiosely, "the new American cooking."

A woman sitting at a table reading a newspaper with both hands while sipping coffee from a straw protruding from a slit in the paper cup's plastic lid caught my eye. I was flabbergasted! I had to ask her why. I introduced myself as a journalist writing about the difference between drinking coffee in Paris and Berkeley. She explained to me that the lid keeps the coffee hot while she reads and that the straw not only cools the very hot coffee as she slowly sips but allows both hands to be free to hold the newspaper and turn the pages. Very practical. Very gastronomically no-no.

I thanked her for sharing her rationale and rushed home to write/draw it up for my magazine. For the illustration, I contrived a home-based, wall-mounted Starbucks coffee-brewing appliance (I couldn't imagine our local-grown Peet's marketing such a device) that would introduce coffee and optional steamed milk directly into the body via an IV drip line or optional oral tube. I have no idea if an IV-drip caffeine appliance is even possible, let alone practical. (I'm pretty sure it's not.) But that's not the point. The image highlights for me the sense of loss of the sensual dimension of coffee I experience in many cafés here. That *sensual dimension of coffee*—its dark good looks, warm feel and organoleptic savor—has been banished behind plastic lids covering paper cups encased in heat-absorbing cardboard sleeves. If IV drip is impractical for caffeine addicts uninterested in the ritual of nursing great-tasting coffee from real cups, they might as well just chew the pulverized beans *à la Balzac*.

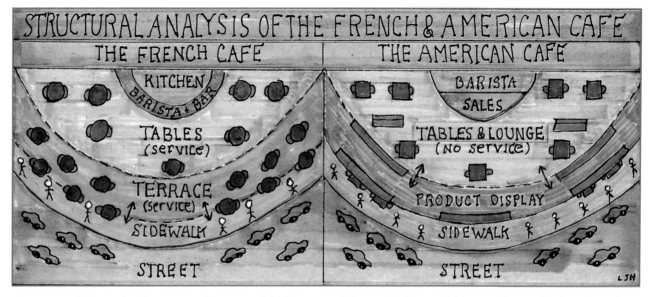

The essence of the French café is service. The essence of the American café (especially chain coffeehouses such as Starbucks and Peet's) is sales. Although the American "to go" café is beginning to offer interior and even exterior seating, there is still no table service and little interactivity between inside and outside spaces. The barista's function at the American café is divided between coffee preparation and product sales (e.g., bulk coffee, coffee-making equipment, branded-logo cups, T-shirts). There are generally no kitchens in American cafés, and any food offered comes from outside vendors or off-site commissaries. The French "sidewalk café" presents an interactive theatrical stage (see diagram arrows) with a kitchen at its center. The American café treats the sidewalk and street as a conduit for commercial activity, virtually cut off from sociability. Once inside the American café, the seated customer is trapped between coffee and product purchases at the counter and merchandise displays at the periphery (see diagram arrows). Two very different cultures, two very different cafés.

A CAFFEINATED TOUR OF THE GHETTO

Down the street from Peet's, at the Cheese Board, very good caps and lattes are made and you can enjoy them at the parklet outside, one of a growing collection of sidewalk bump-outs built collaboratively by the City and merchants to add a soupçon of sidewalk café culture to commercial districts. But the fine Mr. Espresso brand of coffee served at the Cheese Board is offered only in paper cups. *Quelle tristesse!* Well, I say "paper cups" but I know the product is more environmentally appropriate than that and this should but doesn't make me feel better using it.

Across the street at Chez Panisse, the upstairs café (more bistro than café) is not open in the morning and really doesn't function as a Paris café, though that may have been the intention when it first opened above the downstairs gastronomic sanctuary. Although you probably can't order a glass of wine or a cap in the afternoon after the lunch service and hang out for hours writing in your journal, at night you can slip in to one of the little tables in the café's waiting lounge for a quick espresso or glass of wine if the place is not too crowded. Then the café feels to me about as close to a Paris café (in the upscale category) as one can get in Berkeley. Everywhere you look are evocative Marcel Pagnol movie posters mounted on the Craftsman-detailed walls, not to mention Berkeley's best-dressed denizens and our allotment of local celebrities (political, intellectual, artistic) on parade.

Next door at César, a tapas bar/café spun off from Chez Panisse in the 90s, you can go into leisurely afternoon café mode from noon, when it opens, until about 5 p.m. when it starts to fill up with a high-decibel crowd of drinkers and eaters reveling in excellent Spanish delicacies and mixological masterpieces. The coffee is fine and served in ceramic cups. One of the few sandwiches on the menu, the croque señor, is an obvious homage to César's link to the Frenchie restaurant next door—the Chez as we locals call it. But César's croque is nothing like its Gallic inspiration. This Iberian version sports a baguette layered with imported ham and cheese, grilled onions, sliced jalapeño peppers and *allioli*, the Spanish version of French *aioli*. The sandwich is placed in the oven until the bread is toasted and the cheese melted. It's rich and delicious—the perfect prelude to an afternoon siesta.

Across the street from César and Chez Panisse is a café that has functioned in true Paris café mode for decades. It was called the French Hotel café (see Lesson Two) until a recent ownership change. Now called

Vanne Bistro in the boutique Hotel SenS (with an inexplicable and irritating capitalization of the last "s"), many regulars are back following a disappointing renovation. Leonard Pitt, perhaps the café's most celebrated habitué continues to work on his Paris book and film projects from a table occupied on a virtual all-day basis "for the price of two or three cups of coffee," he says. In his most recent book, *My Brain on Fire: Paris and Other Obsessions*, in a chapter devoted to the glories of Paris cafés, Pitt waxes eloquent about the original French Hotel café:

> *None of my friends come to this café. They think it's a dump. And what a glorious dump it is. The French Hotel [café] has not been homogenized, pasteurized and uniformized, and in its imperfections is perfect. This could be an old neighborhood café in Havana. More so when the Latino baristas play their jaunty, brassy Mexican music.*

Havana, indeed! The new owner has given the café a gaudy décor, complete with fake crystal chandeliers and cheap furniture more appropriate to a donut shop in the suburbs (or a bordello, as one customer put it) than an urban bistro/café. The large, illuminated Coke-dispensing machine just does not scream Paris café. Once a regular myself, I can't bring myself to enter unless I need to speak to Lenny. Which is too bad, because the café offers optional ceramic cups and sidewalk tables.

Just north of Chez Panisse, about a block away, is Masse's Pastries, a few doors from our neighborhood's only independent bookstore, Books Inc. You can sit in Masse's with a very good cup of coffee served in traditional café cups. Add one of their delicious croissants, *macarons* or mini fruit or chocolate tarts, and you can imagine you are in a Parisian café/bakery. But there are only about ten seats, and that pleasant buzz of a crowded café that keeps you company while in café mode is limited to a lucky few. It's worth the wait, however, because at Masse's you get not only good coffee and yummy treats, but also pleasant repartee with the Masses.

Between Masse's and Books Inc. is Saul's Restaurant & Delicatessen. Who would ever imagine that a Jewish deli, closer to poet Billy Collins' American coffee shop than a Parisian flâneur's café, would serve as perhaps the fabled gourmet ghetto's most authentic carrier of Paris café tradition, at least in the mornings? I go almost every day for a very good cappuccino and a small breakfast, with a bagel substituting for a croissant.

Saul's cross deli/café pollination is not really so surprising. In his book *A Rich Brew: How Cafés Created Jewish Culture*, Shachar Pinsker describes how in the 1930s Isaac Bashevis Singer installed his European café lifestyle into the Jewish diners and cafeterias of New York's Upper West Side. In my case, it would be how I have installed my Parisian café lifestyle into a Jewish delicatessen in North Berkeley. Spread out over an hour or two of newspaper reading, journal writing and, I confess, texting, my day begins at Saul's very slowly, surrounded by a small group of cordial, buzzing regulars and welcoming, efficient servers. This is the way I like it, whether in Paris or Berkeley, though in Paris the café experience is a truly magical *mise-en-scène* scripted by history, an adrenalized lost-time realm my inner flâneur craves. Here, it's just my life.

THE CURTAIN LIFTS

As they say in France, *vive la difference*! Eventually, after a month or two back home, the ennui-laced curtain lifts and Berkeley's quirky charms, progressive social agendas and natural attractions come center stage. My loving connection to family and friends blossoms forth. Paris flâneur on the Left Bank morphs into Berkeley citizen in the gourmet ghetto. As we say in America, no worries.

It has been said of the Surrealist poet and notorious café habitué André Breton that he was a loner who could not live alone. *C'est moi!* And maybe that's the real secret of the flâneur and his love affaire with Paris, a city where being alone is never lonely. But will I ever make the plunge and move to Paris? I may go to my grave pondering this question. In the meantime, I will take these final pages of *Café French* to Saul's deli and with a Balzacian dose of caffeine coursing through my veins I'll carefully polish my work, dotting all the i's and crossing all the t's. (*Je vais parachever le travail en le peaufinant le mieux possible.*) When I'm finished, I'll start planning my next flâneurian séjour in Paris.

VIVE LE CAFÉ! VIVE LE FLÂNEUR! VIVE PARIS!

A book about the special magic of Paris cafés runs the risk of an implication that café magic cannot be found outside Paris. Au contraire! At the Café Les Deux Garçons in Aix-en-Provence the magic is palpable. Picasso, Cezanne, Zola, Cocteau, Poulenc…they all made this elegant café—opened in 1840 by two partners—their home when in Aix. So did I. I used my fingertip dipped in coffee to paint this portrait.

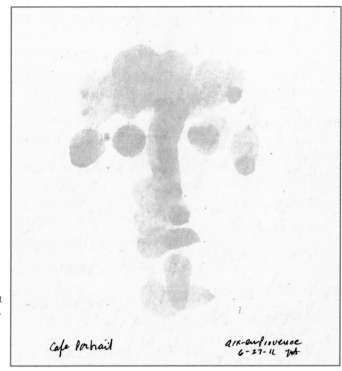

Café Portrait

aix-en-provence
6-27-11

ACKNOWLEDGEMENTS

To all those who have inspired and guided me along my flâneurian path, I wish to express my deepest gratitude: To my grandfather Soloman Hirch Harris (née Arekowitch) and my brother Steven Michael Harris, both of whom introduced me to Paris and its magic as a boy. To my sons, Max and Alex, who I introduced to Paris when they were boys. To Corie Brown and the editors at the late, great online food journal *Zester Daily* for allowing me to express my passion for Parisian cafés with the "Café French Lessons" series. To W. Scott Haine for his extraordinary café scholarship and helpful suggestions. To Susan Griffin for her insights into Paris' demimonde and for her helpful editorial advice. To David Downie for his masterful books about Paris and its gastronomy. To Leonard Pitt for his Paris books and presentations, and our many café conversations. To Paris expat David Jester for his careful edits of the final manuscript, and to his wife Evy for delicious home-cooked meals in Paris. To Lisa Taylor, my French instructor and collaborating linguist. To Terrance Gelenter for introductions to his community of expats and visiting creatives and support for *Café French*. To Lisa Anselmo, author and Paris blogger, for her encouragement and her work to preserve the Parisian café. To Kaaren Kitchell for her café musings and poetic observations. To Tom Farber of El Leon

Literary Arts for his sage advice. To Varda Ducovny, Paris *flâneuse* extraordinaire, for her "getting lost in Paris" strolls through areas of the city I had never seen before. To Jacques and Andrea Valerio for use of their wonderful apartment.

And special thanks to all those who have advised me in the preparation of *Café French* for publication: Agents Kimberley Cameron and Peter Beren; book designer Ashley Ingram; bookseller Marion Abbott at Mrs. Dalloway's Bookstore in Berkeley, Ca.; copyeditor and author Mina Witteman; reader-commenters Sharon Rudnick, Steve Wasserman, Nenelle Bunnin and John Weil; web and social media wiz Ashley Crnkovich; proofreader Molly Stewart; graphic artists Peter Rinzler and Devin Sparks; the helpful crew at Copy Central.

SOURCES

I consulted the following books during the course of my work on *Café French*. These sources represent a very small fraction of the material by historians, journalists, novelists, poets, filmmakers, art critics and memoirists on the subject of Paris, the Parisian café and French culture generally. The blogs, websites and print media I've quoted from or consulted are mentioned in the body of the book.

Travel and Guidebooks

Boyer, Marie-France. *The French Café*. London: Thames and Hudson Ltd, 1994.

Fitch, Noël Riley. *Literary Cafés of Paris*. Washington: Starhill Press, 1989.

Graf, Christine. *The Cafés of Paris . . . a Guide*. New York: Interlink Books, 1996.

Graf, Christine and Dennis, *Café Life Paris: A Guidebook to the Cafés and Bars of the City of Light*. New York: Interlink Books, 2007.

Herbach, Andy. *Eating & Drinking in Paris: French Menu Translator and Restaurant Guide*. New York, 2015.

General Interest

Anselmo, Lisa. *My (Part-Time) Paris Life: How Running Away Brought Me Home*. New York: St. Martins, 2016.

Bradshaw, Steve. *Café Society: Bohemian Life from Swift to Bob Dylan*. London: Weidenfeld and Nicolson, 1978.

DeJean, Joan. *The Essence of Style: How the French Invented High Fashion, Fine Food, Chic Cafés, Style, Sophistication, and Glamour*. New York: Free Press, 2005.

Fitch, Noël Riley. *Paris Café: The Sélect Crowd*. Brooklyn: Soft Scull Press, 2007.

Flanner, Janet. *Paris Was Yesterday 1925-1939*. London: Virago Press, 2003.

Gelenter, Terrance. *Paris Par Hasard: From Bagels to Brioche*. Paris: Paris Through Expat Eyes, 2010.

Levy, Harriet Lane. *Paris Portraits: Stories of Picasso, Matisse, Gertrude Stein, and their Circle*. Berkeley: Heyday Books, 2011.

Marrinan, Michael. *Romantic Paris: Histories of a Cultural Landscape, 1800-1850*. Stanford: Stanford University Press, 2009.

Pinsker, Shacher. *A Rich Brew: How Cafés Created Modern Jewish Culture*. New York: New York University Press, 2018.

Pitt, Leonard. *Walks Through Lost Paris: A Journey into The Heart of Historic Paris.*
    Berkeley: Shoemaker & Hoard, 2006.

Pitt, Leonard. *My Brain on Fire: Paris and Other Obsessions.* New York: Soft Skull Press, 2016.

Sante, Luc. *The Other Paris.* New York: Farrar, Straus and Giroux, 2015.

Sciolino, Elaine. *La Seduction: How the French Play the Game of Life.* New York: St. Martin's Press, 2011.

Shelly, Henry C. *Old Paris: Its Social, Historical, and Literary Associations.* London: Andrew Melrose, 1912.

Tomkins, Calvin. *Marcel Duchamp: The Afternoon Interviews.* New York: Badlands Unlimited, 2013.

White, Edmund. *The Flâneur: A Stroll through the Paradoxes of Paris.* New York and London:
    Bloomsbury Publishing, 2001.

Scholarship

Bachelard, Gaston. *The Poetics of Space.* Boston: Beacon Press, 1969.

Benjamin, Walter. *Selected Writings*, Vol. 4, *1938-1940*. Cambridge: Harvard University Press, 2003.

Dutton, Denis. *The Art Instinct: Beauty, Pleasure, and Human Evolution.* New York and London:
    Bloomsbury Press, 2009.

Gluck, Mary. *Popular Bohemia: Modernism and Urban Culture in Nineteenth-Century Paris.*
Cambridge: Harvard University Press, 2005.

de Goncourt, Edmond and Jules. *Pages from the Goncourt Journals.* New York: New York Review
of Books, 1962.

Haine, W. Scott. *The History of France.* London: The Greenwood Press, 2000.

Hanson, Ellis. *Decadence and Catholicism.* Cambridge: Harvard University Press, 1997.

Rittner, Leona; Haine, W. Scott; Jackson, Jeffrey H. The Thinking Space: *The Café as a Cultural Institution in
Paris, Italy and Vienna.* Farnham, England: Ashgate, 2013.

Robb, Graham. *Balzac: A Biography.* New York: W. W. Norton & Co., 1994.

Rowan, Jamin Creed. *The Sociable City: An American Intellectual Tradition.* Philadelphia: University of
Pennsylvania Press, 2017.

Spang, Rebecca L. *The Invention of the Restaurant: Paris and Modern Gastronomic Culture.*
Cambridge: Harvard University Press, 2000.

Graña, Cézar. *Bohemian Versus Bourgeois.* New York: Basic Books, 1964.

Literary

Balzac, Honoré de. *Treatise on Elegant Living* (First published in French in 1830). Cambridge: Wakefield Press, 2010.

Baudelaire, Charles. *The Flowers of Evil*. Boston: David R. Godine, Publishers, 1982.

Huysmans, Joris-Karl. *Against Nature* (First published in French in 1884). New York: Penguin Books, 2003.

Proust, Marcel. *Swann's Way* (Volume 1 from *In Search of Lost Time*, 1913). New York: Random House, 1992.

Zola, Émile. *The Belly of Paris* (First published in French in 1873). Oxford: Oxford University Press, 2007.

Gastronomy

Beard, James; Alexander Watt. *Paris Cuisine*. Boston: Little, Brown and Company, 1952.

Curnonsky (Maurice Edmond Sailland). *Traditional Recipes of The Provinces of France*. New York: Doubleday & Company, 1961.

Deighton, Len. *Ou Est Le Garlic: French Cooking in 50 Lessons*. New York: Harper & Row, 1977.

Downie, David. *A Taste of Paris: A History of the Parisian Love Affair with Food*. New York: St. Martin's Press, 2017.

Fisher, M. F. K. *Two Towns in Provence: Map of Another Town and a Considerable Town*. New York: Vintage Books, 1983.

Muhlstein, Anka. *Balzac's Omelette: A Delicious Tour of French Food and Culture with Honoré de Balzac*. New York: Other Press, 2010.

Steinberger, Michael. *Au Revoir to All That: Food, Wine and the End of France*. New York: Bloomsbury Press, 2009.

Tower, Jeremiah. *California Dish: What I Saw (and Cooked) at the American Culinary Revolution*. New York: Free Press, 2003.

Wells, Patricia. *The Paris Cookbook*. New York: HarperCollins Publishers, 2001.

Online

Wikipedia, s.v. "Rake (stock character)," last modified February 14, 2019, https://en.wikipedia.org/wiki/Rake_(stock_character)

Online Etymology Dictionary, accessed from July, 2018-March, 2019, https://www.etymonline.com/

ABOUT THE AUTHOR

A native of Los Angeles, California, L. John Harris studied art at the University of California at Berkeley from 1965–1969. In the 1970s, while working part-time jobs in some of Berkeley's notorious food businesses—including the Cheese Board, Chez Panisse and The Swallow café—he wrote *The Book of Garlic* (Holt, Rinehart and Winston, 1974) and became a garlic activist. Harris launched garlic festivals coast-to-coast, including the annual Chez Panisse Bastille Day garlic festival with Alice Waters and was featured in Les Blank's celebrated 1979 documentary, *Garlic Is As Good As Ten Mothers* (Criterion Collection).

In the 1980s Harris published over forty cookbooks with his company, Aris Books. Then, shifting his focus in the 90s to documentary filmmaking, he wrote and co-produced *Divine Food: 100 Years in the Kosher Delicatessen Trade* (1997) and the Emmy-nominated PBS special *Los Romeros: The Royal Family of the Guitar* (2000).

Returning to his art passion in the 2000s, Harris published *Foodoodles: From the Musuem of Culinary History* (El Leon Literary Arts, 2010), which contains 90 of his "foodoodle" cartoons. The book won a Bay Area Independent Publishers Association (BAIPA) award for Best Graphic Memoir. From 2010–2015

Harris was a contributing writer and illustrator for the award-wining online food journal *Zester Daily*.

Today Harris writes articles about food and art, doodles in Paris cafés and operates the non-profit Harris Guitar Foundation in collaboration with the San Francisco Conservatory of Music. He is currently working on a book about the history of Berkeley's "gourmet ghetto."

The author working at Café Madame in 2014.

OTHER BOOKS BY THE AUTHOR

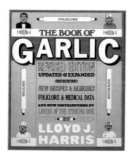

The Book of Garlic (1974)

"Admirably researched
and well written."

–Craig Claiborne *New York Times*

"Highly entertaining."

–Gourmet

"Thick…fascinating and a little crazy."

–Chicago Tribune

The Official Garlic Lovers Handbook (1986)

"Now, with the Handbook, [Harris']
garlic obsession could affect an even
broader audience."

–Alice Waters, from the *Preface*

"A young American, L. John Harris,
developed an obsession that brought
about the American garlic revolution."

–Sue Kreitzman, author of *Garlic*

Foodoodles: From the Museum of Culinary History (2010)

"At every image I laugh, or take initial
umbrage, or think Harris has gone
too far, or not far enough, but I
always end up loving them."

–Jeremiah Tower, from the *Foreword*

"Dark, clever, Dada, absurd—
the humor here is fun to chew on."

–Les Blank, filmmaker

"Amusing, light… your food doodles
say much more than they seem to."

–M. F. K. Fisher

Café

JARDIN

La fontaine rue de Courier

Big Sunglasses

Lunch at the Grand Jussieu
Viande de l'Aubrac

David loves this café --
La fontaine, right around the
corner of his apartment. He loves
the old wall across the street at
the Jardins des Plantes and he
knows all the folks that work
at the cafe.